eBay Business Advanced

All You Need to Know to be Successful Selling on eBay

Contact me at

E-mail: hi@nickvulich.com
Blog: indieauthorstoolbox.com

Amazon Author Page:

- amazon.com/author/nickvulich
- amazon.com/author/nicholasvulich

Publishers Disclaimer:

This book was originally published as eBay 2015. If you previously purchased eBay 2015 you already own this book.

Why you need to read this book

The only thing that's certain when you're selling on eBay is change. Policies change at least twice a year, so do item categories.

The newest elephant in the room is eBay's announcement that both eBay and PayPal were hacked. Over one hundred million user ID's are at risk. Every time user's sign in they are reminded they need to change their passwords. If they want to buy or sell anything they hit a brick wall until they change their password.

For most people that's a little scary. If you're a worry wart it's likely to send you scurrying off to another site like Amazon, Etsy, or Bonanza.

The real stickler is eBay's not doing anything to make it better. They're not doing anything to comfort buyers. They're not telling buyers or sellers here's what we did to make buying and selling on eBay safer. Here's what we did to safeguard your financial information with PayPal.

The other big hurt for eBay sellers is Life Lock. They're all over the airwaves advertising—Hey! Look what happened to eBay and PayPal. You're at risk, but not to worry, we're here to help you. That's what sellers need eBay to do. But, they're not doing anything. eBay's sitting there closed mouth, not saying anything about the breach, while our sales go to merchants on other sites.

Why am I telling you this? because no one else will. They're afraid you won't buy their book if no one's buying anything from you. I'm not going to lie to you.

It sucks, but…

If you're already selling on eBay, odds are you're already feeling the pain. If you're new to eBay and reading this book for advice on getting started, keep in mind—selling on eBay doesn't mean you aren't going hit some icy patches now and then.

Most books that talk about selling online paint this rosy picture telling potential sellers once you post your items for sale on eBay, you can spend the rest of your time lying around the house in your jammies or undies watching TV while the money rolls into your PayPal account 24 / 7.

I wish I could tell you it was so, but that'd be a bit like tossing you under the bus.

I will tell you after you've been selling on eBay for a while it gets easier. You'll make more sales, and many buyers will return to buy from you over and over again—if you give them good value for their money, and great customer service.

Keep in mind—it's a roller coaster ride, no matter how long you've been selling on eBay. Sales vary by season. Normally the summer months—June through August are the slowest time, the Christmas season—November through January is traditionally the strongest selling period. Many eBay sellers earn fifty to seventy-five percent of their profit during the holiday season. Where your sales fall on the scale depends upon the types of products you sell.

Ideally you'll be able to develop a product mix that helps balance sales out so you don't experience extreme seasonal fluctuations. It won't happen magically though. It's something you will have to plan for and work into your marketing mix.

Sometimes you'll have a situation where you've been selling the same product for five or ten years, and all of a sudden sales stop, and the market goes dead for what you're selling. When this occurs you need to be able to assess the situation quickly and determine what happened. Did a new competitor come into the marketplace and undercut your prices? Was a new product released that makes yours obsolete? Are there too many sellers offering the same products you're selling?

Whatever you do, you need to react quickly? Otherwise it's like beating a dead horse. You'll never get anywhere.

Hopefully you've got a Plan B. And, that's what this book is all about. We're going to teach you about how to sell on eBay today—and tomorrow. To do that successfully you need to be able to move from Point A to Point B without tripping over your own two feet.

Keep in mind, nothing I'm going to teach you here is new. This book isn't going to walk you through listing your items on eBay. There are plenty of other books that do a great job of that.

You should also know I haven't discovered any hidden secrets I'm going to share with you. Selling on eBay isn't rocket science. It takes a lot of hard work, and some good old common sense.

If you can execute in five key areas, you'll have everything you need to succeed in online selling—today, tomorrow, and into the future.

1. Plan for success
2. Establish a Niche
3. Ship like a pro
4. Sell international
5. Know your numbers

Table of Contents

Seller Standards – Are You Meeting Them

Beginning in August of 2014 eBay implemented a set of standards sellers are expected to maintain.

The crazy part is sellers with five star feedback can be penalized or have their selling privileges restricted or revoked if they run afoul of certain standards.

How can this be, you ask? Let's examine a few examples.

Many sellers offer their product line across multiple platforms. Some sellers use software or apps to sync all of their items, sales, inventory changes, etc. Other sellers attempt to go it alone and make the changes themselves.

Suppose something goes wrong.

You make an error, and forget to take an item down. Your automated app allows something to slide by. Now suppose an item sells, and you need to cancel the sale because you're out of inventory.

That's a penalty shot under the terms of eBay's new seller standards.

Suppose a customer contacts you to say they don't want to complete a transaction. If you initiate the return eBay considers it a seller issue and you are penalized with a seller defect. As a result of the new seller standards you are forced to choose between offering good customer service, or telling your customer, "Sorry. I'd like to help, but you need to contact eBay to get the ball rolling."

Think it can't happen?

About eight months ago I imported four thousand items from my Amazon store into my eBay store using an export service. Somehow they brought in hundreds of previously sold items, along with the current items in my Amazon store. I've been fighting to eliminate all the dead items since then, but in the meantime I've had to cancel eleven sales.

eBay's new seller standards don't go into effect until August, but they reach back up to one year for data to enforce those standards. As a result, I'm in peril of losing my Top Rated Seller status or having my ability to sell on eBay restricted for infractions that happened well before the new policy went into effect.

What makes it worse is I have nearly 19,000 positive feedbacks with no negative or neutral feedbacks. My DSR rating for the last ninety days is 5.0 out of 5.0. The only thing that's changed is eBay has decided to evaluate sellers based upon different standards.

It's crazy, but true.

Here's the way eBay describes the new seller standards, "Sellers who provide the great service that creates better shopping experiences and repeat sales stand to benefit from the update to seller performance standards."

The first evaluation for sellers takes place on August 20, 2014. If you've completed more than 400 transactions in the last three month period, you are evaluated based on that three month period. If you completed fewer than 400 transactions in the past three months, you are evaluated based upon your sales for the previous twelve months.

If you're curious how you're doing in meeting the new seller standards visit your seller dashboard. It shows trending data on how your performance stacks up.

What this means is eBay no longer evaluates your performance based upon your four DSR ratings, instead they evaluate your performance based upon your **defect ratio**.

Seller defects are defined by eBay as occurring in the following situations.

1. A 1, 2, or 3 star rating on DSRs.
2. A DSR of 1 for shipping time.
3. Receiving negative or neutral feedback.
4. A return with the reason listed "item not as described."
5. Having a buyer protection case opened for the reasons "item not received" or "item not as described." (Buyer protection cases you settle, or that are settled in your favor do not count against you.)
6. Seller cancelled transactions.

To qualify for unrestricted sales on eBay sellers must maintain a defect ratio under five percent. To qualify for Top Rated Seller Status sellers must maintain a defect ratio under two percent.

The biggest takeaway is –

Buyers won't be able to see your defect rate, but the higher your defect rate is, the lower your items will be shown in search.

What that means for sellers is if you have a high defect ratio, eBay will move your items to the bottom of search results, or they will not show them altogether.

The net result is fewer sales.

Check out this link if you want to learn more about eBay's seller standards.

http://pages.ebay.com/sellerinformation/news/springupdate20 14/sellerstandards.html

. . . .

Before I go any further let me tell you a little more about me, so you can understand why I'm the right guy to help you grow your eBay business.

Why Listen To Me

Hey there, Nick Vulich here.

If you're like me, I'm sure you're probably a little skeptical about taking advice from someone without knowing a little bit about them first.

I've been selling on eBay since 1999. Most of my online customers know me as history-bytes, although I've also operated as its old news, back door video, and sports card one.

I've sold 30,004 items for a total of $411,755.44 over the past fifteen years, and that's just on my history-bytes id. Right now I've cut way back on eBay selling to focus on my writing, but I still keep my hat in the game. That way I can stay current with the challenges my readers face every day when they go to sell on eBay.

I've been an eBay Power Seller or Top Rated Seller for most of the past fifteen years, which means I've met eBay's sales and customer satisfaction goals.

This is the eighth book I've written about selling on eBay. The first two, *Freaking Idiots Guide to Selling on eBay*, and *eBay Unleashed*, are aimed more towards how to get started selling on eBay. *eBay 2014* is directed at more advanced sellers and tackles many of the challenges top rated sellers face in the eBay marketplace. *eBay Subject Matter Expert* suggests a different approach to selling on eBay – building a platform where customers recognize you as an expert in your niche, and buy from you because of your knowledge in that field. *Sell It Online* gives a brief overview of selling on eBay, Amazon, Etsy, and

Fiver. *How to Make Money Selling Old Books & Magazines on eBay* talks specifically about what I know best, how to sell books and magazines on eBay. *eBay Bookkeeping Made Easy* helps sellers understand how to keep track of the money they are making, and how to take advantage of the tax code to make even more money.

eBay 2015 is an attempt to tie it all together. For those of you who've been following along and reading all of my books, some of this is going to be a rehash. The section on bookkeeping is taken directly from my book *eBay Bookkeeping Made Easy*. It's not the entire book, but enough to give you a good primer on what it's going to take to run an eBay business. Some of the materials in the sections on shipping and international selling are excerpted from my book *eBay Shipping Simplified*. Again, it's info you need to know and apply today to thrive on eBay.

The majority of this book—over 125 pages of it are new to this book, and will help you make the most of selling on eBay.

My goal is to help you become as successful as you wish to be.

Let's get started...

Make These Changes First

From my experience selling on eBay there are certain actions sellers can take that will help them become more successful.

If you're a seller teetering on the brink of success instituting some of these changes could give you the extra nudge you've been looking for to break into the big time. If you're a new seller, there's no better time to get started doing things the right way. You don't have any bad habits to break. Just jump in and get started.

Keep in mind—this is stuff that has worked for me with the items I sell. Not every idea will work for you. Keep doing what works for you—adjust, or discard the rest.

1. Remove all HTML code from your listings.

eBay's Cassini Search does not play well with HTML code—especially when you have HTML code in the listing header.

I love a fancy listing template that has a great design and perfectly formatted pictures, but what I like even better is listening to the cash register ding on my eBay app.

If your sales are down, and nothing you do is working—strip the header out of a few listings, strip all of the fancy formatting and templates out of a few more. Then see what happens.

If unformatted listings allow you to make more sales, that's the way to go. By doing this you can decide for yourself what works and what doesn't.

2. After you post a listing check it out on your smart phone and tablet. If you have trouble viewing your listing re-work it, or cancel the listing and start over.

The internet today is all about mobile. People constantly check their phones, tablets, and kindles all day long for new emails, tweets, and Facebook updates. Last Christmas nearly thirty percent of holiday shopping took place on mobile devices. This year that number is expected to be closer to fifty percent.

If your listing isn't optimized for mobile, you're going to miss out on fifty percent of the customers searching for your items.

At the end of the day when you're done listing items, check some of your listings using your smart phone or iPad. Ensure that your items appear in search, and they're optimized for mobile viewing. If you inserted your photos into your listing using HTML code or a listing application like Auctiva or Ink Frog your pictures are going to appear small and they will be hard to view. If you posted them using eBay's list your item page pictures will expand to fill the entire device screen, and potential buyers will be able to use the arrow keys to move between one picture and another.

Ask yourself which format you're more likely to buy from, and make the appropriate changes.

3. Get straight to the point. Less is better. People are in a hurry to get things done. The easier you make it to buy from you, the more stuff you're going to sell.

People are lazy. They read auction descriptions the same way they read blog posts and everything else on the internet. They scan the description for words that catch their fancy. They cruise through bullet points for a quick overview. They glance at the captions for pictures.

If they run into a big blob of text, they're going to click the back arrow button and move on to the next listing. White space, bullet points, and bold headings are your allies in making more sales.

4. Include more and better pictures.

A good fifty percent of buyers make their decision just by looking at the pictures in your listing. They don't have time to read, or they don't want to read your item description. Many foreign buyers can't read or understand your description. They rely solely on the pictures you include to make their decision.

Some sellers play to this. They include lots of close up pictures, and encourage buyers to check the pictures and decide for themselves if the item meets their needs.

5. Focus on the 80 /20 rule. Concentrate on selling the 20% of items that bring you the most profit. Scrap the slow sellers.

If you're like most sellers, a few of your items account for the majority of your sales volume.

If you've got an eBay store the odds are you have hundreds, maybe thousands of items languishing in there. Maybe ten or twenty sell every month, but the rest of them just sit there—festering. They suck up your monthly free listings, and cost you additional listing fees. They taunt you into working extra hours hoping they'll be that one extra sale you need to buy a new iPhone or an extra appetizer at lunch.

Quit playing the longshots. Take aim, and start focusing on sure things. Concentrate on the twenty percent of items that sell the best, don't waste time and money on listings that rarely sell.

6. Don't try to reinvent the wheel. It's great to find a new product no one else has that will sell like hotcakes. There are very few items like that. If you focus all your time on looking for the newest greatest item you're going to miss out on a lot of sure things.

Everyone wishes they could go back in time and be the first guy in on the Hula Hoop craze, the Pet Rock, or the Chia Pet, but—those kinds of things are a one in a million shot. If you concentrate all of your effort on the long ball, you're gonna miss the sure hits along the way.

Sure…catching the wave on a new fad can make you rich and famous, but selling sure things like denim jackets, vintage toys, etc. will keep the cash registers ringing day in and day out. They'll put food on the table, and gas in your tank.

Chasing fads will suck up listing fees, time you could spend posting profitable items, and free time you could have invested with your family and friends.

7. Don't beat a dead horse. Items run out of gas. They stop selling for one reason or another. Know when to call it quits and move on to a new niche.

Good things come to an end.

I've spent the last fifteen years selling vintage magazine articles, prints, and advertisements. They've been slugging along in low gear since the recession of 2008. eBay's move to fixed price listings is another nail in their coffin. Sales are down, selling prices are down, and profits are down.

I'm beating a dead horse.

I've got two choices—reinvent myself, or reimagine my product line. It's hard. We've been together for fifteen years. There's still money coming in—sometimes thousands of dollars a month, but it's nothing like it was.

The challenge for 2015 is to reinvent my business and carve out a new niche.

What about you? If you're beating a dead horse, do you have a plan to put it down, or breathe new life into it?

8. Spend more time on customer follow up. Chit chat. Talk your listings up. It's going to help you build a relationship with customers, and sell more stuff.

Getting to know your customers doesn't take long. You just need to make it a regular part of your business day. When someone inquires about an item you have for sale—answer their question. Take a few minutes to thank them for contacting you. Talk up your item, and your product line. Ask how they're going to use it, and what other items they'd like to see you offer.

If it's close to a holiday—wish them a "Merry Christmas!" or a "Happy Easter!" If you want to be politically correct, wish them a "happy holiday season." Getting to know your customers only takes a few moments, but it gives buyers a warm and fuzzy feeling about doing business with you.

9. Try new things. Complacency has killed more businesses than anything else. Try selling at least one new product every week. At the end of the year if only five of them work, you've still got a stronger product line.

Products and entire product lines go stale. Things become obsolete. People become obsolete if they don't change. Think back to the guys you knew in high school and college. How many of them are still reliving their glory days? It's great to spend five or ten minutes with them and reminisce, but then you start to get this queasy feeling—this guy's not going anywhere. He's stuck in the past.

Products are the same as people. They get stuck in a certain time period.

If you're not selling nostalgia, you need to cut the strings and try new things. It will make your product line stronger, and force you to become a better seller.

10. When a buyer protection case is filed against you, put aside any personal feelings, or any thoughts the customer is trying to put one over on you. Pull the trigger, and give them a full refund—especially with low dollar amount items. You'll feel better, and it'll make you look better to your customers and to eBay.

Think of it this way. In the larger scheme of things— what's twenty, fifty, even a hundred dollars compared to everything you sell on eBay? You may be in the right. The customer may be hosing you, but—is it worth lowering your ranking in search, or having your selling privileges restricted or revoked?

Probably not.

Look at the big picture, and do what's right for your business. Don't let personal feelings knock you down.

11. Take some extra time off—just for the heck of it. Selling on eBay is demanding. Customers are after you 24 / 7. You're rushing to list new items, and to ship old ones before your 24 hour deadline expires. Take a break now and then to make time for yourself.

Selling on eBay is a tough racket. It never stops. There's always one more item to list, one more package to mail, and one more email to answer.

It'll tear the hell out of you if you let it, and make you old before your time.

Be sure to schedule some time for yourself before you become the ogre in your basement dungeon.

12. Sell for charity.

eBay Giving Works makes it easy to sell for charity. Pick a national charity like the Red Cross, or pick a local charity that's close to your heart.

Add two or three charity auctions to your repertoire every month. It'll make you feel better about selling on eBay. It'll make your customers feel better about buying from you, and it'll make you more money.

Not every Giving Works listing sells, or sells for a higher price, but they do get a lot of page views. My normal listings receive twenty to twenty-five page views. When I add a charity to the listing it draws several hundred page views, especially when I list using a large national charity.

Even when the item doesn't sell, that's a lot of extra eyes on my listings. Many of those lookers take a peek through my eBay store; some of them are likely to pick up an item or two as they're cruising through.

If you haven't tried it yet, list a couple of your items with eBay Giving Works. It just might become a habit.

Plan for Success

Too many sellers rush into eBay without a plan.

They jump in and start selling before they understand what the market is all about. Other newbies are sloppy, and post poorly lit pictures, or write vague descriptions that don't really tell buyers anything about what they're selling. Too often, sellers overprice, or underprice items in their haste to get their listings posted. If they overprice their item it doesn't sell, so they decide eBay doesn't work. It's just another scam that stole their money. If they underprice their item, and it sells, they complain because they can't make any money.

. . . .

Selling on eBay is part art and part science.

I can teach you the science or the mechanics of selling on eBay, but to be really successful you need to understand the art of selling on eBay, or what I call gut instincts.

When you're scouting inventory you've got to be able to walk through a room and instantly zero in on the money items.

I sell books, magazines, and paper memorabilia. When I hit an estate sale, on my first round through the house that's all I'm looking for.

The first thing I look for is vintage magazines. I've got a mental list of about twenty-five titles I always buy, but what really excites me is when I come across something new;

something I've never seen before; the more pictures they have in them, the more I want them.

I'm also scanning the room for items I don't normally sell, but things I think would complement my product line. Here's the way I look at it. If you see something totally new and unique that appeals to you, it's going to have the same effect on buyers in your niche.

I think Mike Wolfe on American Picker's put it best, "If you see something different, and it's the first time you've ever seen it, you better buy it."

If you don't have that gut instinct to recognize something good—it's going to be harder to be successful on eBay.

Here's why?

If you don't have that gut instinct to recognize what's good and what's not, it's going to be like walking into a room with blinders on. There may be fifty items that will allow you to double or triple your money, but you're likely to miss every single one of them, because you're laser focused on just a few items you're comfortable selling.

That's good for the guy behind you. He's going to grab everything you walked by, and he's going to be able to pay his bills this week.

But it sucks for you.

You're going to be right back to thinking eBay is a scam, and there's no way anyone's making any money on the site. It happens every day. Don't believe me? Just hop on any eBay forum and get a whiff all of the bitching and whining. Need a little more convincing? Stop by the Ecommerce-Bytes Blog and check out some of the comments for any of their eBay related articles. It's the same people—constantly whining about how horrible and mean eBay is, and how they can't make a dime anymore because of that old Scrooge—Mr. Donahue.

Guess what?

It's not eBay. It's you. It's your attitude.

The sooner you understand whether you make or lose money on eBay is all about you and how you approach selling, the sooner you'll find the success you're looking for.

Let me tell you a story.

I was a salesman covering a four state area (Iowa, Illinois, Missouri, and Wisconsin) for more years than I care to remember. Most of the time I did this I also sold historical memorabilia and sports cards on eBay. I popped listings up in between trips and phone calls, and I wasn't doing half bad. Most months I made $1500 to $2000 profit, $5 to $10 at a time.

One day I received a call from the VP of Sales. My position was being eliminated, but not to worry. They were offering a severance package, they wouldn't contest my unemployment, and they'd give me a good reference. Of course, they did need one small favor in return—I had to sign a paper promising not to sue them for any of this.

What do you do?

If you want the money, you have to sign. To make a long story short, I signed the papers. I put work behind me, and decided I was going to make a serious run at eBay.

If you tuned me out for reminiscing, here's where you might want to start listening again.

I decided to make a serious run at selling on eBay.

By most standards I was already making good money. Fifteen hundred to two thousand dollars a month isn't pocket change. The thing is: If I was going to make my living on eBay I needed to double or triple that number before my unemployment and severance pay ran out. That gave me roughly six months to go from so-so to oh-boy.

To do that required some serious planning.

Making Your Plan

Anybody can make a few sales on eBay. The key to success is to keep those sales growing while at the same time discovering new products to sell and new avenues to make your offerings available through.

Doing this isn't as easy as it sounds.

To be successful selling on eBay, or anywhere else for that matter, you need to have a plan, and you need to work your plan.

For me, one of the hardest parts of making a plan was already filled in. I knew what I wanted to sell—historical memorabilia and collectibles. So, I knew the what.

I also knew the where. I wanted to sell my items on eBay.

That left the who, the why, and the how. If I planned on being successful I needed to connect all of the dots.

That meant answering the who's.

1. Who are my customers?

2. Who is my competition?

I needed to answer the why's.

1. Why do customers buy the stuff I sell?

2. Why should these customers buy from me, instead of from another eBay store?

I also had to understand the how's.

1. How do I list my items for maximum impact?

2. How am I going to ship my items—both economically and safely?

3. How am I going to find a steady supply of products to sell so I can keep my business growing?

To put together an effective business plan, you need to answer all of the above questions.

I was lucky. I already knew what I wanted to sell. A lot of sellers who are new to eBay stumble when they're asked that question. For many new sellers, uncertainty about what to sell is the major stumbling block that keeps them from becoming successful.

I'm going to cover that topic in much more detail in the section about how to discover your niche. For now were going to concentrate on answering the other questions posed above.

Who Are My Customers & Why Should They Buy From Me

If you're already selling on eBay, it's going to be much easier to answer these questions. The best way to do this is to ask your customers directly. Every time you send out a customer service email, include a brief survey.

It can be as simple as,

Thanks again for making your purchase from history-bytes. We realize you have lots of options to choose from when purchasing historical collectibles on eBay, so the fact you chose to do business with us is a great honor.

Please take a few moments to check your items over carefully when they arrive, and make sure they meet your expectations. Should you have any questions or concerns please feel free to contact me personally. I will be happy to do whatever I can to make it right for you.

Could I also ask a small favor?

Here at history-bytes we're always trying to make your shopping experience more enjoyable. Would you have a few moments to tell us about your experiences with history-bytes, and why you chose the particular items you did?

It will help us accomplish two important tasks:

1. It will help us ensure a pleasant shopping experience for our customers.

2. It will help us to select more products that our customers want and need.

To make it as easy as possible, just click reply to this email and tell us what you like or don't like about shopping with history-bytes. Next, tell us a little bit about why you purchased your item, and how you intend to use it. Finally, tell us what other items you'd like to see us carry.

Thanks again for making your purchase from history-bytes. If you were able to make time for our survey—you're amazing. Rest assured we'll use that info to make your shopping experience with history-bytes even better.

Have a great day!

That's all there is to it. Take our survey. Make it your own. Feel free to change it up a bit and personalize it for your business. Ask about specific products, different parts of the shopping experience, or what customers liked or didn't like about your eBay store or listings.

You'll be surprised what you learn. It just may help you rocket your sales to a new level.

. . . .

If you're new to eBay and don't have any customers to survey you're going to have to work things a little differently. Most of your research is going to focus on analyzing sales trends and using your gut instincts to determine how that data affects you.

The first thing you need to do is conduct an advanced search for items similar to what you plan on selling.

If you've never run an advanced search before—don't panic. It's super easy to do. Look for the search box at the top of the eBay page. Just to the right of it you'll see the word "advanced." Click on it.

This will take you to the advanced search page. I know, it seems overwhelming at first, but there are only a few areas of it you need to use.

The most important thing you need to understand is the only information that counts is what you find in sold listings. Anybody can list anything they want to on eBay and ask for a crazy amount of money. The way we separate the wheat from the chaff and get to the good stuff is by only analyzing completed sales where people spent money to buy something.

This tells us the seller did something right with their listing.

If you're with me so far let's get started.

Pick an item you're interested in selling and run an advanced search. Count how many items sold in the last thirty days (hint: they're listed in green). Now count how many didn't sell (hint: they're listed in red). Divide the number that sold by the total number of items that were listed. This will give you the percentage of items that closed successfully. The most recent number I've seen is 42% of auction listings posted on eBay sell successfully.

Hopefully, the number you get will be somewhere between 40% and 50%.

Now it's time to dig deeper into the items that sold.

- Were they listed as auction or fixed price?
- What was the high and low selling price?
- What was the average selling price?

- Did the auction listing use buy it now? If so, how many buyers used buy it now to purchase the item?
- Did the fixed price listing use best offer? If so, how many buyers used it to buy the item?
- What prices did sellers start their auction listings at?
- How many pictures did sellers use in their listings?
- What keywords did sellers use in their titles? What keywords did sellers use in their descriptions?
- How was the item description worded? Did the seller use bullet points? Lots of white space? Or, lots of description?
- Did the seller offer free shipping?
- Did the seller use flat rate or calculated shipping?
- What was the average shipping price?

These are just a few of the questions you want to ask yourself as you're researching your market. The more information you have, the easier it's going to be to pick items that sell, and craft superior item descriptions.

The next thing you want to do is checkout your competition.

If you followed through with the exercise listed above you already discovered a number of sellers in your potential niche. Run another advanced search for an item you are considering selling.

This time visit their eBay store.

Check out the design first. Do they have a custom storefront? Do they have a custom listing header with categories and search features? Do they have store categories set up (usually there's a category list to the left of the store items)? Are they using promotional boxes to feature their items or shipping rates?

This is going to give you some good general information, and help you to understand what you're up against. Take a look at how many feedbacks each seller has, and record the name of the top five sellers. You may even want to sign up for their store newsletters. This will help you do some strategic spying on your competitors.

When you're finished looking at the store, click into some of the categories and see what items sellers are offering. How broad is their product line? Do they sell at the low or high end of the price spectrum? And, finally—how many items are they offering in their store?

It's a lot of information, but by the time you're done— you're going to know a lot about your competition.

The next part of your plan is to put it all together. Examine what your top three to five competitors are doing. Look at their price, their shipping charges, their product line, and the way their items are listed.

Ask yourself –

1. What products aren't they offering that buyers in your niche would want?
2. What products, services, or features can you add to the mix that would make you stand out compared to these sellers?
3. Do you want to compete on price? Service? A broader product line?

4. What shipping strategy do you need to use—free? Low price? Etc.?
5. What tone do you need to set in your listings to attract buyers away from your competitors? Do you need to be serious, humorous, or just offer a more complete listing?

It's a lot of work, but if you do it all—you're going to know your competition, and what it's going to take to attract buyers to your eBay listings.

Uncover Your Niche

The real key to success on eBay today is to cultivate a niche and carefully grow it by adding a steady stream of new products.

A lot of people get started selling on eBay by selling everything but the kitchen sink. They sell spare items they find around the house. Then they begin selling items they find at garage sales, yard sales, and estate sales. Sometimes it works, but it's a tough sell because it's hard to get repeat customers when you're selling a mish mash of stuff.

To really be successful you need to build your tribe of fanatical customers who keep returning to your eBay store to see what's next? You need them to keep asking themselves, what crazy or unique item did this guy find now?

If you can develop even one hundred regular customers who check back every week or every month for new items you're going to be extremely successful selling on eBay.

. . . .

The definition of a niche is a subset or small portion of a larger market.

For example—clothing isn't a niche. Women's clothing isn't a niche. Plus sized women's work suits, or plus sized women's swimwear is a niche.

Books aren't a niche. Books about Western Americana are a very general niche. Antiquarian books about Western bad men are a niche, as are vintage illustrated children's books.

Ideally your niche should be in an area you enjoy and have at least some knowledge of. You're going to be spending a lot of time with it. The more you know about your niche, the products in it, and how to determine their condition the easier it's going to be to source and sell products.

....

When I first started selling on eBay I was all over the board. I sold old clothes, unwanted household items, etc. After that I started specializing in movies on DVD and VHS, and then vintage sports cards from the 1950's and 1960's.

I made a lot of sales, and I had some repeat buyers, but I wasn't making a lot of money. I bought the videos online from wholesalers in 100 and 500 case lots. Many of the movies would sell for $2.00 or $3.00 each. I paid $1.00 each so I was making a few bucks. After a couple months I'd package up the movies that didn't sell into lots of 25, 50, or 100 and start them at 50¢ each. That allowed me to break even on the dogs, or make a few cents on them.

I soon learned movies were a large market on eBay, but they were too competitive for me to make a decent profit.

Sports cards were another market I made a lot of sales in.

Early on I determined to concentrate on fifties and sixties baseball cards with a sprinkling of football cards. Over time I developed a strong following of customers.

I wasn't really doing anything special. I'd buy "lots" and "partial" sets on eBay and Yahoo. I'd break them up and resell the individual cards for one to ten dollars each. Every few months I'd package up the cards that didn't sell into lots organized by team or year.

I made a lot of small dollar sales and developed a strong following of regular customers, but I never hit a home run. I couldn't make a living on what I was doing. It was more like a hobby that paid dividends.

I was stuck. I didn't have the money to move up to the big dollar cards, and I didn't want to remain a bottom feeder forever, so I cut the cord—disposed of my inventory, and moved on.

. . . .

It was about that time I discovered a guy selling magazine articles on eBay. It seemed sort of crazy, but I followed his listings for a while, and he was making some decent sales. Nothing to write home to mom about, but…it appeared to me there was an opportunity to take it a few steps beyond what he was doing.

I poked around eBay to see if any other sellers were doing the same thing, and he pretty much had the market cornered at that time. There were several sellers offering vintage magazine advertisements and prints. One or two other sellers were hawking vintage car literature, advertising, and service manuals.

What I saw convinced me there was an opportunity here. I picked up an 1865 issue of Harper's New Monthly Magazine on eBay for fifteen bucks, and jumped in. My fifteen bucks turned into $250, and over the next year it grew to over $10,000 in sales.

Even though I didn't know it for quite some time, I had stumbled into a profitable niche. Several years later I was interviewing for a sales position at a car dealership. After some discussion about what I did on eBay, the sales manager came out and asked me how I got the idea.

"You stole it from someone else, didn't you?" I just nodded my head, waiting to see where he was going with this.

"It's ok," he continued, "the best ideas are the ones we borrow."

He was right. I stole the idea, but I refined it and developed it into a unique niche by specializing in history, biography, and science. Over time I added vintage prints, war of 1812 newspapers, and Spanish American War prints.

My niche was a work in process. It was, and still is, constantly evolving based on customer needs, and new products I stumble across.

That's the story about how I got started in my eBay business. $411,000 in sales later it's starting to implode on me. The economy is some of the problem. My biggest buyers were universities, museums, libraries, researchers, and small publishers. A good deal of their funding dried up after 2008. Changes in the eBay platform took their toll, especially the move away from auction listings. The influx of fixed price listings made most of my items nearly impossible to discover in search.

A smart seller would have thrown in the towel years ago, but I kept rebuilding my broken brand, attempting to breathe new life into it.

It's still good for a few thousand dollars a month, but…the writing is on the wall. Next year I'll be back selling in a newer more profitable niche.

. . . .

Here are a few ideas to help you discover your niche.

1. Take your time. Many sellers stumble across the perfect niche like I did. Keep an eye on what's selling well on eBay, Amazon, and other ecommerce websites. Watch the news and TV entertainment programs. Follow blogs and read your local newspaper.

Even better, just watch the people around you. Grab a seat in the food court at the mall and really listen to what people are talking about. Watch which stores they visit, and which ones they avoid.

The majority of people couldn't spot a new trend if it reached out and smacked them in the face. We don't notice them until they're firmly planted in our living rooms. That's why so few of us made a killing with Microsoft, Apple, AOL, or any of the other high tech companies. Trends just sort of nudge their way into our lives. At first they are invisible, and later on they became common place.

A niche is a lot like a new trend. It's right there in front of you every day. It's just hard to see until you open your eyes, and let it in.

2. Make sure your niche has enough potential customers to keep you busy, and make the income you're looking for. If a niche is too narrow or specialized, you're going to run out of people to sell to.

Here's an example of what I mean. When I first started selling on eBay, there was a guy selling back issues of several publications from the State Historical Society of Iowa. He was getting $15 to $30 an issue, and was making ten to fifteen sales a week. Not too bad.

I did a little more digging and discovered the State Historical Society had a huge trove of issues and would sell you as many as you wanted for 50¢ or $1.00 a copy.

That's a nice profit margin, but…the potential was limited. The market for Iowa history on eBay was too small. It offered a good part time income for this one seller, but it wouldn't work on a larger scale.

Unless. I contacted almost every historical society in the United States, to inquire about the cost of back issues. A few states like Missouri and Wyoming offered back issues at prices similar to Iowa. Most states asked at least $5.00 per copy. Others like California recognized the value of what they had, and priced them accordingly at $10.00, $20.00, or more per copy.

That confirmed it wasn't a profitable enough niche to build a real business on. Keep this in mind as you're searching for a niche, because the sooner you find it's a bust—the more time and money you'll save.

3. You need to have a ready supply of new product available to fuel your growth.

You can find the hottest niche out there, but if you can't get your hands on enough products to sell, you're not going to make it. If you're selling vintage product, there needs to be enough of it available for you to have a ready supply. If you're selling a handmade craft or other product, ask yourself if you can supply enough products profitably to make it worthwhile. If you're purchasing product to resell from a wholesaler look at all of your costs and ensure you can charge enough to recoup your costs and a respectable profit.

Don't just look at your item cost. Consider how much shipping to you and to your end user is going to be. Think about how much wiggle room you have on price. When you first start selling a new product, you might be the only one offering it, or there may be just a few of you, but as your niche grows—more and more sellers are going to jump in.

One problem I had selling magazine articles was my inventory cost virtually nothing, but because of the volume of listings I ran—my eBay fees were out of this world. eBay fees could easily add $8.00 to $10.00 to an item that cost me 25 cents or less.

New sellers popped up every few months and soon faded away, because they didn't understand the real cost of making a sale. They assumed because the initial cost was cheap—they could undersell me, offering the same product for $5.00 or $10.00. The economic truth was…they lasted three to six months and disappeared from eBay.

You need to have a ready supply of product available, and you need to be able to sell it at a profitable price otherwise you won't succeed.

4. You'll hear many eBay sellers say you need to corner the market on your niche to make it on eBay. I'm not so sure about that. If there's no competition for the products you want to sell it can only mean two things, either it's a totally new product never before seen, or there's no market for it—other sellers have tried it and given up.

If you research your market and there's no one else out there selling the same product or niche on eBay, you need to ask yourself why.

It may be there is a limited supply of product available, or a limited demand. It may be too new for enough people to know what it is. It may be too difficult to ship, or too expensive to ship.

Before you jump into a niche make sure you investigate it thoroughly, and completely understand it.

Sell a few products, and slowly test the waters.

5. Make sure your niche is broad enough to let you expand and add new products over time.

I started out selling magazine articles. As time when by I slowly added prints, vintage newspapers, and other paper items. Several times I built niche stores offering rock n roll and sports memorabilia.

Make sure your niche is big enough to add new products and expand to new markets. Keep testing new items, and if they sell well, consider opening a new eBay store that caters to your new niche.

It's not easy to find and build a niche, but it is the most profitable way to sell on eBay. When you've hit the right niche you won't have to look for customers, they'll come looking for you.

Ship Like a Pro

U nderstanding how to ship the items you sell is just as important as knowing which items to sell.

Online sellers are going to be faced with two different types of shipping situations: domestic (shipping within your home country) and international (shipping outside of your home country). Many sellers spend years trying their hardest to avoid making international sales because they're afraid of the extra paperwork involved or that there may be excessive damage claims, theft, or negative feedback caused by shipping or communication glitches.

The truth is international shipping is no more difficult than domestic shipping. It's just a matter of learning and getting used to the extra paperwork involved.

Domestic Shipping

Most of the shipping you're going to do is considered domestic shipping, or shipping within your home country.

The first thing you need to understand is the Post Office offers many different ways to ship items. The shipping method you choose depends upon the item you are shipping, its size, value, and how quickly you want it to arrive.

Here is a breakdown of the most common shipping services available from the post office, and the different items you can ship with them.

- **Media mail** is designed to ship books, CDs, DVDs, and other educational materials. Media mail does have a few restrictions. Material cannot contain any advertising pages, so most magazines are ineligible for media mail shipping.

  Packages sent by media mail are subject to inspection by the Post Office, so if you do include ineligible items, they can send the items back to you postage due. The main advantage to sellers from using media mail is it's cheaper to ship heavier items like books. As a result, you can offer your customers a less expensive delivery option. This is especially important if you are selling in the book category, because eBay requires sellers to offer an option priced at $4.00 or less.

  Delivery time is normally 3 to 8 business days, but can vary based on the season. At Christmas time it can take as much as two to three weeks to deliver a media mail package so be sure to give buyers a heads up – "Hey. It's cheap, but it's slow." That way they understand it's the post office, not you.

- **First Class**. If you're shipping smaller items (less than 13 oz.) first class is going to be the most economical method available. You can ship just about anything— books, clothes, DVDs, CD's, jewelry, stamps, post cards, you name it. The problem is tracking is not available on all first class packages, so you cannot offer proof of delivery.

If you're mailing flat items like baseball cards and postcards then you cannot add tracking. Your package is required to be a minimum of 1/8" thick. Delivery time is normally 1 to 3 days depending upon where you are sending your package.

- **Priority Mail**. The majority of items sold by online sellers are shipped by priority mail. It has several advantages over other services including:
  1) You can mail heavier items than first class,
  2) Most items are delivered within 1 to 3 days, and
  3) Tracking is available on all packages, so you have proof of delivery for eBay and your customers, and
  4) The Post Office provides free shipping materials so you don't have to invest in boxes and other expensive packaging materials.
  5) You can schedule a pickup and the post office will send a carrier to your home or business to pick up your packages.

The disadvantage to using priority mail is that it is more expensive than first class or media mail.

- **Priority Mail Flat Rate** takes the guess work out of shipping. You can ship whatever will fit in the package regardless of the weight anywhere in the United States for a preset fee. This is a great option for buyers and sellers because it's less expensive to ship heavier items, or multiple items that will fit into a single package.

Like regular priority mail—it's quick, offering 1 to 3 day delivery, comes with delivery confirmation, and packaging materials are free from the Post Office. Be sure you use the Flat Rate Priority Mail boxes when using this service.

- **Standard Post** is a less expensive option for mailing parcels and oversize packages. The normal delivery time is 2 to 8 business days. Tracking is included in your shipping fees.

- **Express Mail** offers overnight delivery service to most areas in the United States. If your customer needs an item quick, this is the service for them. Be aware it's expensive and the fees are based upon the size and weight of the package you are sending.

    Like Priority Mail, Express Mail offers free packaging materials and delivery confirmation. Sellers also receive $100 dollars of insurance free with most parcels sent, and signature delivery confirmation which eBay and PayPal require on more expensive packages.

- **Priority Mail Express Flat Rate** offers next day delivery (in most areas), plus the added convenience of simplified rates. When you use the flat rate boxes anything you mail in them (regardless of weight) ships for one fee, so if you're shipping heavy items—this is the service for you.

If you want to get the full scoop on these delivery services check out the following link.
https://www.usps.com/ship/compare-domestic-services.htm

Package Your Items Like a Pro

How you package the items you sell makes a major difference in how buyers view you as a seller.

If you just toss your items into a box or envelope it's going to leave a sour taste in the minds of your buyers. Their purchases are likely to arrive damaged or with bumped and scuffed up packaging that looks like it's been run through the ringer.

I know many books recommend recycling used boxes, packing materials, and such to use in your shipping. In my mind—that's the worst mistake you can make.

You only get one chance to make a good first impression. If your package arrives all scuffed up, or with all sorts of squiggly lines where you crossed out previous addresses, customers are going to be concerned about their purchases. If that's the way you package stuff, your buyers are going to think "God help me" about the stuff you put inside the box.

Set Up Your Shipping Station

Most sellers I've worked with ship their items from the same desk they sell from. If you're a part-time seller, that's okay. If you eBay for a living I'd recommend a separate shipping station.

Here's why.

Shipping is a specialized task. To do it right you need a lot of space and all of your packaging materials and supplies close by. I have a separate desk and table set up for shipping. My shipping computer is only used when I'm shipping items or tracking shipments. It's an older castoff, but it serves the purpose. I have two printers hooked up to it…a Zebra LP 2844 and a Samsung laser printer.

Most of my shipping labels get printed on the Zebra. I use the laser printer to print packing slips and thank you cards. I also have a postal scale that attaches to the computer through the USB port. It's digital and can accurately weigh up to twenty-five pounds in one ounce increments. The weight is automatically transferred into Stamps.com with one click of my mouse so there's never any guess work involved. I normally round up to the next ounce to add a little wiggle room for tape or the label.

I have sturdy warehouse shelving set up opposite to my desk. The bottom row has flat boxes in various sizes. The next shelf has priority mail boxes and envelopes. The shelf above that has stayflat mailers and padded mailers. The top shelf has all of my miscellaneous supplies—shipping labels, paper, extra rolls of tape, box cutters, and Sharpie markers.

Everything is close by. Once I get started I can normally package and ship thirty or forty items in an hour and I'm done. Before I had my shipping station it always took twice as long because I was running from here to there looking for stuff, or trying to find a good spot to spread all my stuff out.

Must Have Supplies

There's certain equipment and supplies you need to keep on hand so you can ship smart.

>> Packaging material. Make sure to stock up on boxes, padded mailers, stayflat mailers, bubble wrap, and tape. The worst thing that can happen is to be in the middle of packaging up your orders, and then discover you don't have the supplies you need.

If you ship priority or express mail stop by the post office and pick up the supplies you need. Better yet, hop on line and check out https://store.usps.com/store/browse/category.jsp?categoryId= shipping-supplies.

Order your boxes ten, twenty-five, or more at a time depending upon how quick you go through them. The post office will deliver them free within two to three days.

If you need to purchase boxes, padded mailers, or stayflat mailers—consider Uline - http://www.uline.com/. They have decent prices and quick delivery.

Wal-Mart carries a great selection of boxes in their shipping supply aisle. The prices are good, especially when you compare them to the big box office supply stores.

I've also had good luck buying supplies from several suppliers on eBay.

. Value Mailers
http://stores.ebay.com/VALUEMAILERS?_trksid=p2047675.1
2563

. Royal Mailers

http://stores.ebay.com/Royalmailers?_trksid=p2047675.l2563

>> **Postal scale**. If you sell online you need a postal scale. I know a lot of sellers try to fudge it and just guess at weights. Trust me. No one is that good. Every ounce you guess wrong costs you at least seventeen cents. Over the course of a year that's going to easily be a hundred bucks or more.

Best advice: buy a good digital scale. You can find them with weight capacities starting at five pounds. I recommend choosing a scale from USPS.com. They have a good selection and the scales hold up well.

>> **Printer**. The printer you use is a matter of preference. I like to use a Zebra label printer because it prints a small compact label you can peel off and stick on your package. There's no messing with tape, or ink cartridges because it's a thermal printer. The next best choice is a laser printer. The ink is less expensive, and it prints quicker. There's nothing more aggravating than waiting for a slow ink jet printer to finish printing your label. The last choice is an ink jet printer. It's slow, but it will get the job done. If you use adhesive backed labels an ink jet printer is your best bet. Whenever I tried them in my laser printer they were too thick and jammed it up.

>> **Shipping tape**. I usually pick up my tape at Sam's Club or Wal-Mart. You can buy single rolls or save a few bucks and buy them in six packs. My only recommendation is not to buy the

cheapest tape you can find. It tears, it splits, and it's a mess restarting the roll.

>> **Bubble wrap**. If you're packaging china, old books, or other fragile items you're going to need bubble wrap. Here's one item it's okay to reuse. Good places to purchase bubble wrap are Sam's Club, Wal-Mart, or online.

>> **Box cutter**. Be sure to keep a couple of box cutters and plenty of extra razor blades on hand. You want to package your items right, and the best way to do that is to give everything a snug tight fit. To do that you need a box cutter with a sharp blade so you can easily refit boxes.

>> **Peanuts** are those little white foam half circles shippers use to line their packages. They're all static filled and stick to everything. I hate them and refuse to buy anything else from sellers that use them. Use peanuts at your own risk, they're a sticky mess.

Packaging Tips

Okay. You've set up your shipping station and stocked up on supplies. Now it's time for *Packaging 101.*

The best tip I can give you is to always choose the right type of packaging, and err on the side of more packing materials, not less. This is one area you don't want to skimp on.

Tip #1. Choose the right type of packaging. If you're shipping a newer book or a paperback it's okay to use a padded mailer. If you're shipping a rare book or vintage book you need to package it differently. Use a box and make sure it is placed inside a sealed plastic bag, and then wrapped with newspaper or bubble wrap. This does two things: it keeps the corners from getting scuffed or bent, and it protects the book from moisture damage should your box be exposed to water.

If you're shipping china, glass figurines, or other fragile materials pick a box about six inches larger all around than what you are shipping. Line the box with bubble wrap or wadded up newspapers. Next wrap each item in bubble wrap or newspaper and tape it up so it is secure. Lay the item in the box and cover it with bubble wrap or newspaper. Continue doing this until the box is full. Build another layer of bubble wrap or wadded up newspapers at the top. You'll know you've got it right when you shake the box. If you feel stuff shifting around open the box and add more packing material.

When you ship electronics, laptops, or tablets, your best bet is to ship them in the original box. If that isn't possible, find a box just slightly larger than the item you're going to ship. Build a nest in the box using foam, bubble wrap, or wadded up newspapers. Place your item in a sealed plastic bag, to prevent moisture damage. Wrap it several times with bubble wrap. Place the item in the box. Wrap any accessories, discs, power cord, etc. separately and place them in the box. Build a nest around the top of the box before you seal it to ensure the item will not be shaken in transit. Tape all of the way around the circumference of the box, length wise and width wise. This ensures that the tape won't break free where the box can come open in shipment.

If you're shipping clothes you can pop a shirt or t-shirt into a priority mail bag. If you're shipping jackets, jeans, or multiple items use a flat rate priority mail box to reduce your costs. If you're unsure which is cheaper—regular priority mail or flat rate, weigh it out and let the numbers do the talking.

I'm not going to describe anymore scenarios, just understand that you need to adapt every packing situation to the item you are shipping.

I've received close to a thousand packages over the last fifteen years. Some of them were perfectly packed, some were adequate, and quite a few arrived banged up and had the items I purchased hanging half way out of the box or missing.

Tip #2. The best time to decide how to pack an item for shipment is before you list it.

Think about it. If you list a computer, or rare figurine—how are you going to determine shipping charges if you don't know how you're going to pack and ship it?

In my case I have hundreds of rare newspapers dating from 1806 to the Civil War period, but I don't have a cost effective way to ship an individual paper to buyers. If I fold the paper to make the size manageable, I would ruin a good part of the items collectability. To ship a single paper would require me to buy an oversized casing for it, and then a custom box to put it in. Packaging could easily run forty to fifty dollars before shipping costs. That's a hefty chunk of change to add to a paper I'm selling for twenty-five dollars.

The economics don't work out in this case, so the papers remain in my private collection for now.

Make sure you're not going to go underwater on the items you sell. Before you list an item assess what it's going to take to ship it. What kind of packaging materials do you need? How much is shipping likely to cost? Is the item expensive enough to require insurance? If so, how much is that going to cost?

Know what you're looking at up front, because after the sale you can't come back and ask the customer for more money.

A lot of sellers box their items up at the time they list them. They weigh the package, input the weight into the eBay shipping calculator, and all of the hard work is done. If and when the item sells they grab the box, print a label and drop it in the mail.

I say to do whatever works for you.

Just keep in mind buyers always have questions. You may need to open the box up to answer a question or to shoot a quick picture or two. Also, not every item sells. You may need to bundle that item up with several other items to make a sale.

Do I Need To Offer Free Shipping

Free shipping is the biggest bugaboo facing online sellers right now.

eBay encourages sellers to offer free shipping and they promote items with free shipping to buyers, because of this many new sellers think they have to offer free shipping. Let me assure you: that's not true.

You don't have to offer free shipping on any of the items you sell. However, you may want to offer free shipping. Here's why?

Normally sales increase when you offer free shipping. There's something about "free" and "shipping" that makes buyers loosen up their purse strings and spend more money. I'm not sure what it is but the word "free" is one of those magical keys that can get consumers to pull the trigger and spend more money.

Keep that info tucked away in the back of your head for a moment.

Just because eBay likes free shipping and consumers like free shipping doesn't mean it's the magical ingredient you've been searching for to increase your sales and profits. It needs to be the right combination that's good for both of you. That means you need to be able to make a profit, and your customer needs to get a good value when you offer free shipping.

How does that work?

If you're selling light weight, easy to ship items free shipping should be a no brainer. Let me repeat that. If you're selling light items you can ship in an envelope or padded mailer and ship for under a dollar you are probably better off giving your customer free shipping rather than trying to charge them that buck. So if you're selling postcards, baseball cards, small knickknacks, and inexpensive jewelry items that you mail in a regular envelope—mark your item up a buck, and give your customer free shipping.

If you're selling heavier items, low margin items, or custom made items free shipping may make sense. Before you pull the trigger though, do your research. Investigate what other sellers with similar items are doing. If everyone else is offering free shipping you're going to be better off following the pack, unless…and, this is a big unless. If everyone else has marked their item up enough to cover shipping, plus a couple extra bucks for profit it might make sense to charge shipping, and price your item as low as you can while still holding a decent profit.

If the majority of sellers in your category are split with some offering free shipping and some charging for shipping you may want to test the waters. Offer a few items with free shipping, and a few with your regular shipping charges. Run with the method that makes the most sales for you.

If you're the only one selling a certain product and you're making a killer profit, go ahead and give your customers free shipping. It's like extra icing on the cake. It's one more reason to buy from you.

One of the better discussions I've found on the web about free shipping was written by Katen Raj on *CPC Strategy*

Blog. Give it a look if you need a little extra help working through this issue. http://www.cpcstrategy.com/blog/2012/04/the-free-shipping-formula-for-online-retailers/

Setting Shipping Rates in eBay

S etting shipping rates is another tricky area that can confuse sellers.

Here's the least you need to know.

- If you're a Top Rated Seller or want to be a Top Rated Seller you're required to provider tracking information for all of your domestic sales. You are also required to post tracking information back into the listing on a minimum of 90% of the items you sell.
- Top Rated Sellers are required to ship all of their items with a one day handling period.
- If the value of any item you sell is over $200 you are required to provide signature delivery confirmation.

If you're not a Top Rated Seller and don't have any intention of becoming one it's still a good idea to provide delivery confirmation on every item you send. It protects you from bad buyers who may open an item not received case because they know they will win if you can't provide proof of delivery.

Now we'll get down to the nitty-gritty of setting up shipping in your item listings.

To set your domestic shipping options look for the section labeled *add shipping details* on your sell your item form.

The first choice you need to make is to select your shipping method from the drop down box. There are four possible choices: flat cost, calculated, freight, and no shipping—

local pickup. Flat cost is where you charge all buyers the same shipping rate. Calculated shipping uses the eBay shipping calculator to figure shipping based upon your item weight and where it is being shipped to. Freight is for larger items too big to ship by the USPS or UPS. Items shipping by freight are carried by a semi or common carrier.

If you sell large items that need to ship by common carrier keep in mind that eBay's freight calculator only works up to 150 pounds. If your item exceeds that weight you need to use flat rate shipping. You also need to understand a few things about truck lines. Most carriers only require their drivers to pull your item to the back of the truck. It's up to your customer to have people available to help them get their item out of the truck and carry it inside the house.

You need to explain this to your customers in your listing description, and again in the shipping instructions you send the buyer after the sale. Here's another tip. You can request the truck line to call your customer the day before delivery. Sometimes they will do it; sometimes they don't, so try not to make too many promises.

To set up calculated shipping click the blue lettering that says *calculate shipping*. This will open a pop up box. Fill in the options, and you're good to go.

If you're using flat rate shipping, click in the box that says standard shipping. Select the shipping service you want to set up, and enter the shipping fee in the smaller box to the right where it says cost. If you want to offer free shipping for that service put a check mark where it says free shipping. To offer more shipping options click the blue lettering that says *offer additional service*.

To offer local pickup, check the box where it says *Local Pickup*. Be careful when you select this option because local pickup is not available in all categories.

Think long and hard before you offer local pickup for your items. Do you really want to invite customers into your house? Over the years I've had a number of local buyers insist on picking up their items to save on shipping. Most times I've delivered the items to their business or met the customer outside of McDonald's or another local business. It's less risky, but a major pain in the backside.

Best advice: avoid local pickup whenever possible.

If you set up flat shipping rules you can check the box to apply them. If you would like to setup or edit your rules, click on the blue lettering that says *edit rules*. The pop up box will walk you through setting up shipping discounts. Keep in mind if you edit the top set of rules the changes are only good for the listing you are currently working on. If you want to create a discount for all of your listings you need to scroll down to the bottom of the pop up box where it says Promotional Shipping Rule (applies to all items).

If you haven't used this feature before I would suggest giving it a whirl. You'd be surprised at how many buyers will shop for additional items to save a few bucks on shipping.

The next choice you have is to select the *handling time*. If you're a Top Rated Seller you are required to ship all items within one day so be sure to select that option.

The final item gives you a nudge to add next day shipping to your listing. I don't offer the service unless buyers contact me and say they absolutely have to have next day shipping. My reason for not offering next day shipping is very few people request it, and you have deadlines you need to meet to get the item to the post office on time. It takes more effort than it's worth.

That's it. Your shipping options are set.

Here's another quick tip so you don't have to go through this with every item you list—set up one of your listings as a template, or when you list new items pull up one of your old listings and select the option to sell a similar item. When you use either of these options all of your previous info transfers over to the new listings. Use the info you want to keep, type over or delete the unwanted info.

Printing Shipping Labels Using eBay & PayPal

B oth eBay and PayPal allow sellers to print shipping labels directly from their sites. The process is easy to use and allows you to print professional looking labels and invoices to include with your shipments.

Print eBay Shipping Labels

The easiest way to print shipping labels using eBay is to go into your *Selling Manager*. In the left hand column find where it says *Selling Manager Pro*. Just down from there you'll see the word *sold*. Select it.

That's going to bring up a list of your sold items. Locate the item you want to ship, and scroll over to the far right column labeled actions. The first thing you should see is *Print Shipping*.

When you select *Print Shipping* it takes you to the eBay ship your item page. When you click into it the page is prepopulated with all of your item information.

At the top of the page you're shown the item description, price paid, shipping fee, shipping service paid for, and the expected delivery date. The left hand column contains the shipping information—the buyers address and your address.

If you need to make a change to either address, select where it says change, and enter the correct shipping information.

Just below the address details you'll see a box labeled add message to buyer email. I have a standard thank you message in here, but you can use it to tell your buyer a little more about the item, or direct them to your store specials. It's up to you.

The center column contains the package details. It's where you choose the carrier, add shipping options, and choose your mailing date. eBay has two approved carriers the United States Postal Service (USPS), and FedEx. My shipping experience has all been with the USPS so that's what I'm going to cover here. If you ship using FedEx, select them as the carrier and follow the prompts to complete your shipment.

Getting started, the first thing you need to do is select your carrier. In this case choose USPS.

Use the next box to select your shipping service. The choices are priority mail, first class package, parcel select, media mail, and priority mail express. The priority mail and priority mail express options let you choose the level of service you want.

After you've selected your service you have the option of printing the auction number or some other message on the label. If you want to do this check the box, and type in your message. The default message is the auction id.

The final box lets you choose the mailing date. You can choose today, tomorrow, or the next day. The reason for this is you're supposed to mail your package the same day you print the label, so if you're printing the label today, but not mailing your package for two days, you should change the date. I've never had a problem with the post office if I'm a day or two late dropping the package in the mail, but now you know the correct way to do it.

The third column shows your postage cost broken down by the postage cost, the delivery confirmation fee, and the total cost. Below that you have an option to hide the shipping so buyers can't see how much actual shipping cost you. It's your choice—if you're playing by the rules and charging actual shipping, let your buyers see the shipping cost. It will prove you're on the up-and-up.

When you're done click purchase postage. When you do this your PayPal account will be charged for the shipping fees. The next screen will show a mockup of the label. You can print a sample, or print the label.

After the label is printed the program will automatically transfer tracking information into the item listing so buyers can follow the movement of their package as it is being shipped to them.

Alternatively, you can print your postage labels directly from PayPal. To get started open your PayPal account and locate the transaction you want to print the postage for. Click on the text where it says *Print shipping label*. It brings up the same shipping page we used above, so you can follow through using those directions.

Do I Need Insurance

When eBay allowed sellers to charge customers for insurance I required all of my buyers to purchase it. It saved a lot of hassles. If the item was lost, the customer was taken care of.

What I discovered after shipping over 30,000 items is very few items are lost, stolen, or damaged in transit. I think I've had two damaged packages, and three lost packages in fifteen years. So is insurance really necessary? It depends on you, and your tolerance for loss. Most of the items I ship cost between twenty to twenty-five dollars. Insurance costs close to two bucks for each package. Take two bucks times thirty thousand packages and that's close to sixty thousand dollars.

My losses in all this time have amounted to under one hundred bucks. If I'd bought insurance on every item I shipped I'd be out close to $60,000 dollars. When you look at it that way—insuring my packages doesn't make sense.

But...insuring my more expensive packages does make me feel all warm and fuzzy inside. Because of that I decided to pick a number where I would insure my shipments. If the value exceeds that number I purchase insurance. For me the magic number is fifty dollars. For you it may be ten dollars or one hundred dollars. The best I can tell you is to choose your threshold for loss and make a decision to insure all shipments that exceed that number—that way you can sleep nights.

Here's the least you need to know about insurance.

- eBay no longer allows sellers to charge buyers for insurance. You can roll it into your shipping costs, or you can bury it in the cost of your item.

- Filing an insurance claim with the Post Office is a pain in the rear end. It takes a minimum of thirty days for the post office to reimburse you. Many times it can take two or three times that long.

- When you sell something on eBay it's hard to prove the actual value of an item, especially for collectibles and one-of-a-kind items. Just because you paid five bazillion dollars for a rare candy bar wrapper doesn't mean that's the value of your item.

- You may have insurance but your customer doesn't care about that. They don't want to wait thirty days or more to get their money back. If you make them wait for a refund odds are you're going to receive negative feedback.

With all of that said, how do you file an insurance claim? The easiest way is to do it on line. Go to the following link https://www.usps.com/ship/file-domestic-claims.htm. It will walk you through filing an insurance claim for a lost parcel.

Here are a few of the highlights to keep in mind.

You need to upload tracking info for the item, a copy of the sales receipt or your eBay auction listing number (to prove value), your insurance receipt, and if you received a damaged item—you need to save the item, along with all packaging materials until the claim is completed.

If for some reason you can't file the claim on line call (800) 275-8777, and they will send you a claim form.

Using a Third Party Shipping Solution

eBay's shipping label service is great, but sometimes you need a little more oomph to boost your sales and simplify things even more.

I've been using Stamps.com for nearly ten years and it's been a great alternative for me. Other people have had good luck using Endicia to handle their shipping needs. Both services charge a monthly service fee for using them.

I know what you're thinking. Wait a minute Nick, I'm trying to save money, not spend even more.

Believe me, I understand. The thing is I actually save a lot of money using Stamps.com to power my eBay shipping. Here's why I use it, and how it saves me money.

What got me hooked on Stamps.com is it's the only way I can ship my items first class international without going to the post office and having them print labels for me. If you use eBay's shipping solution or Click-N-Ship® you can only ship internationally using priority or express mail. When I do that, international sales go down because of the extra shipping costs involved. The extra sales I get by offering the less expensive shipping solution more than cover the $15.99 monthly fee.

One of the other reason I like using Stamps.com is it collects information from all of the platforms I sell on and lets me handle all of my shipping from one central location. For me, that means I can ship the items I sell on eBay, Amazon, bid Start, and my own website all from the same program console.

I don't have to jump from site to site to ship everything. If I need to look up shipping info for an item—it's all in Stamps.com.

It's convenient. I like that. It's worth the extra fifteen dollars a month it costs me to use the service.

To get started with Stamps.com click on the following link http://www.stamps.com/. Select get started to register for a new account. Most times they offer a sign up special that gives you a free postal scale, $25.00 in free shipping credits, and miscellaneous other goodies, along with a one month free trial.

Once you're good to go you can connect all of your seller accounts.

What I'm going to do next is give you a quick walk through on how to connect your seller accounts, and how to print postage using Stamps.com. (I assume Endicia works similar to this but I've never used that service so I can't provide you with specifics.)

Don't worry. I'll make this quick and painless.

Setup Shipping Accounts

There are two ways to set up your accounts. Select *Manage Sources* in the toolbar at the top of the screen, or select *batch* from the toolbar in the left hand column.

Choose Create Profile, and select the data source you want to create.

Printing Postage

When you open your Stamp.com dashboard there is a command bar running across the top of the screen. There are four main tabs that you'll use over and over again: import orders, manage sources, print, and add order.

- Import orders lets you collect your orders from all of the sites you sell on and bring them into Stamps.com.
- Manages sources lets you add, delete, or edit data streams.
- Add order allows you to print a label for a package where the customer is not included in any of your data streams. An example is when I send out a review copy of one of my books. The recipient is not in my data stream, so I need to set up a one-time shipment.
- Print pulls up the screen to print your shipping label.

Okay let's assume you just sat down at your desk and you're ready to start shipping. What do you do?

Select <import orders> from the top menu bar; you'll be prompted several times about actions that are in progress. Most often Stamps.com wants permission to update addresses to match the official address in the postal system computer. Click okay.

After a little while all of your orders will appear in a spreadsheet in the middle of the screen. Select the item you want to mail, and click on the recipient name. This will open up the shipping screen for that customer.

Off to the left hand side of the screen you will see your name and address. Below that you will find your customer's name and address. You can make whatever changes you need to the shipping address here. The next line is labeled email address. Check the box in front of it and it will populate with your customer's email address. When you check this it will send shipping and tracking info to your buyer. The box right after this is cost code. You can make an internal note here if you are tracking categories for shipping.

The next column contains your shipping options.

If you have a USB scale it will transfer the weight with the click of a button. I usually round up to the next ounce or two depending on the item I'm shipping. That gives me a little wiggle room for the label and tape.

After this you need to choose the type of mail piece— package, thick envelope, etc.

Then you select the mail class –

- First Class
- Priority Mail
- Express Mail
- Parcel Post
- Media Mail

Place a check mark in the tab to select the mail class. When you do this it will show the cost for that service. Some classes are blanked out if you can't choose them to ship that particular item. As an example packages over thirteen ounces cannot be shipped by first class so that shipping method would not be available for you to select.

After this you choose tracking options—delivery confirmation (free with most shipping methods), signature confirmation (an additional $2.35), or none (tracking is not available on flats sent by first class).

Just below this there is a line labeled options. This is where you can add—certified, USPS insurance, registered, or COD delivery.

The next option lets you select insurance. You can select none, or Stamps.com. Your final choice is whether you want to hide the postage cost so buyers cannot see it. If you marked your shipping up a lot be sure to choose this option.

After you've selected all of your options click <save> at the bottom of the box. When you do this a green circle should appear in front of the <order id> on the spreadsheet. To print your postage choose <print> from the menu bar at the top of the screen. You should see a pop up that shows the printer name and details. Select <print> at the bottom of the screen to print your label.

International Shipping with Stamps.com

Setting up an order for international delivery is very similar to shipping a domestic order. The only difference is you need to complete a customs form.

Here what you need to do to fill out the online customs form.

Click on the customs form, and it will display a pop up box for you to fill out. At the top of the form it asks for a phone number. If your customer listed a number with eBay it will prepopulate. If they did not give a phone number I just fill in 999-999-9999, otherwise it will not let you continue.

Where it asks for contents you are given several options. Choose <merchandise>. In the box next to this type a short description. I usually type article or print.

About midway down the page there is a section labeled *itemized package contents*. The first box asks for the quantity or number of items in your package. After that you're asked for a short description of the item. It should prepopulate from your eBay item description. If the description is too long you need to shorten it, or the form will not process properly. The next item it asks you for is the weight of just the item (without the packaging).

When you've completed all of the items the box at the end of this line asks *add item*. Check that box, and it will move your description into the box below that line.

At the bottom of the pop up box is a form you need to check. It begins with "I acknowledge..." Once you select the check box, the pop up box disappears, and you can print your item like normal.

Sell International

H ere's a secret many online sellers don't know. The fastest growing sellers on eBay are powering their growth with international sales. According to a recent article on *Linnworks*, "76% of [the] fastest growers are primarily trading across borders."

The beauty of selling internationally is when the domestic economy slows down and sales in your own country become sluggish, there are still pockets of growth and increasing demand in foreign economies. The key to tapping into these growth pockets is to make your items available to sellers in those countries.

I started listing items internationally in 2001, and within a year thirty to thirty-five percent of my orders were shipping overseas. Over the last fourteen years I completed nearly 5,000 international transactions with only two lost packages.

If you're on the line about getting started with international shipping—consider baby-stepping it. Start with proven foreign trade partners like Canada, the United Kingdom, and Australia. There are few language barriers dealing with these countries. You should also consider selling to Germany. According to a recent article in *Forbes Magazine*, Germany and the United Kingdom account for 48 percent of all international sales made on eBay.

. . . .

To qualify for international visibility on eBay sellers must meet several standards.

- Have a verified PayPal account tied to their eBay seller account
- PayPal must be offered as a payment option
- Must have 10 or more positive feedbacks
- Items must be listed in the appropriate category
- Need to enable shipping to countries you want to ship in
- For best visibility sellers must specify the levels of shipping service they are offering

The other great thing is if you sell using your eBay.com account your feedback will be visible to sellers on eBay's foreign sites.

If you are a seller in the United States and specify you will ship to Canada, your items will automatically be listed on eBay.ca.

Items listed on international sites do not count as duplicate listings, so sellers are not penalized for listing the same item on different eBay sites.

. . . .

eBay gives you four ways to make your items available to international buyers.

1. Opt into eBay's Global Shipping Program.
2. Enable your items for international shipping.
3. List your items on international sites.
4. Open eBay stores in countries where you do a large amount of business.

What I'm going to do next is look at each option in more detail and explain who it is for, and how you can get started using it.

eBay Global Shipping Program

Several years ago eBay introduced their Global Shipping Program. It's an easy way for sellers to jump into international selling without having to worry about shipping rules, customs forms, etc.

If you've been itching to get started with international sales, but were afraid of the extra work involved I suggest giving it a shot using eBay's Global Shipping Program.

Many small sellers are terrified of international shipping. They've heard so many horror stories they're scared to give it a shot. They don't want to fill out customs forms, or worry about whether their package is going to make it all the way to Timbuktu or not.

eBay has eliminated all of that grief for sellers who use their Global Shipping Program. Sellers list their items just like they normally would. When the item sells they ship it to an eBay shipping center in the United States.

Bing badda boom! As soon as it arrives at the shipping center, your responsibility for the shipment is over. From that point on eBay and their shipping partners assume all responsibility for getting your package to its destination.

Here's how it works.

When you list your item for sale on eBay check the box to include your item in the Global Shipping Program and you're good to go.

Some categories don't qualify for inclusion in the Global Shipping Program. When you bump into these eBay will flag the item and let you know. I do a lot of selling in the collectibles category. Collectibles manufactured before 1899 don't qualify, so I see this issue pop up quite often. The only way around it is to ship the item internationally yourself. I'll discuss this option in more detail later.

When an item sells using the Global Shipping Program sellers can't send the buyer an invoice. eBay takes care of all this for you. The reason is you have no way of knowing what their shipping fee will be.

Once the customer pays you will receive your payment notice along with the address to ship your item to. An easy way to recognize a payment made through the Global Shipping Program is the address will include a long reference number.

Ship your item like you normally would. Include delivery confirmation so you can be sure the item was received at the shipping center. Once you have confirmation the item was received, your part in the transaction is complete.

eBay's shipping partner—Pitney Bowes—will readdress the item, fill out all of the appropriate customs forms, and ensure your item is delivered to the customer.

That's the way it should happen. Every now and then things don't work out as planned—the customer doesn't receive the item, or it arrives damaged. As a seller you're supposed to be protected from receiving negative feedback in such a situation. That's true to a point. You need to keep an eye on your feedback profile, and keep after eBay to update it when errors are made.

I received a negative feedback due to a customer not receiving their item. I knew it wasn't received, because that's what the seller wrote in his feedback. So I called eBay customer service and explained the problem. After about fifteen minutes of researching the problem the rep agreed I was not responsible. He removed the negative feedback while we were still on the phone.

If you experience a similar problem contact eBay customer service immediately. When you call have the listing item number and the feedback information available and ready to share with them. Make it easy for eBay to help you.

Overall the Global Shipping Program is a great way to increase your sales. At my peak selling period international sales accounted for roughly thirty-five to forty percent of my eBay sales and profits.

If you're looking for an effortless method to grow your sales opt into the Global Shipping Program and give it a shot.

Enable Your Items for International Shipping

We've already talked about eBay's Global Shipping Program and how easy it is to use, so why would anybody want to ship international packages on their own?

That's a great question.

It comes down to having more control over your shipping options, and the ability to make more sales. When you use eBay's Global Shipping Program they figure in custom's fees, a markup to pay themselves and their shipping partner an additional profit, plus actual shipping costs. The final number eBay shows your customer for shipping can be mind-boggling, and can cost you the sale.

Let me use the products I sell as an example. When I ship items internationally on my own I charge $5.00 to ship items to Canada, and $9.00 for shipping anywhere else in the world. Sometimes I make a few extra bucks, sometimes I lose a few bucks, but over time it averages out. Keep in mind, the buyer is still on the line for duty and customs fees when their item arrives.

When I sell the same item using eBay's Global Shipping Program they charge my customer in the low twenty dollar range for Canada, and in the low thirty dollar range for Europe and the rest of the world. My items normally sell for sixteen to twenty-five dollars, so customers are confronted with some serious sticker shock when they're hit with eBay's shipping price.

Self-preservation is one of the major reasons I ship most international packages myself.

What I'm going to do now is walk you through setting up the international portion of your eBay sell your item form. It's structured very similar to how you set up your domestic shipping options so it should be easy to follow along and use.

. . . .

Everything you need to set your international shipping options can be found in the box labeled *International Shipping*.

The first choice you are offered is to opt into the Global Shipping Program. In this case you want to leave that box unchecked.

Below this you have a drop down box that offers you the option to select flat rate, calculated shipping, or no additional options. As a quick review flat rate shipping is where you have one set shipping fee for all buyers, calculated shipping uses the eBay shipping calculator to determine the shipping price based upon where you are shipping your item to. The difference is— flat rate shipping is easier to set up and use, but calculated shipping can give buyers closer to you a break in shipping costs thus giving you the opportunity to grab additional sales from price conscious buyers.

After you choose your shipping method you'll see another drop down box that says shipping. It gives you three choices: worldwide, chose custom location, or Canada. I normally set up a separate price for worldwide and Canada— anymore is overkill in my book. However, if you ship a lot of packages to Mexico, the UK, or wherever go ahead and set up a special price for them too. The drop down box next to this lets you choose the type of service you wish to offer, and the box to the right of that lets you set your shipping price.

Below this you see a line labeled *offer additional service*. You can use this to offer shipping to an additional location, or to offer a different delivery method.

In the *additional ship to locations* you can check off areas you are willing to ship to and the buyer can contact you for more details. Some sellers have lots of rules about where they will and will not ship too. A lot of sellers mark Malaysia, Italy, Mexico, Russia, etc. off limits because it's all over the internet that other people have experienced problems when they ship packages there. In my book that's all talk. I've shipped items to all of those countries and never had a problem. All I'm saying is if you're going to put areas off limits or discourage buyers from certain regions wait until you have a problem with the area, then evaluate the situation and determine how you want to handle it.

The final line—combined shipping discounts, lets you apply your discount rules to this purchase if you set them up. My items are light and generally only add a few ounces to the package therefore I ship all additional items for free. It's a great way to encourage buyers to continue shopping with you. If you can't offer to ship all additional items for free—consider offering some type of discounted shipping for additional purchases. It will bring you more business over the long haul.

That's it. You're open for international business. Sit back and wait for the orders to role in.

I'm going to make one additional suggestion here. Take a few moments to help set buyer expectations. International buyers are similar to domestic buyers—they want to purchase their items today and receive them yesterday.

Most times shipping goes smoothly and items arrive on time, but there are many circumstances that are beyond your control, especially when you're dealing with international customers.

I normally post the following information in each of my listings and include it again in my shipping emails.

"Normal international delivery time is eight to fifteen business days, but it can take as long as four to six weeks—depending upon customs and other shipping issues. Please be patient, and take this into consideration when placing your orders."

It helps to set buyer expectations before the order is placed. That way if the customer asks where their item is you can refer them back to the info posted in your listing. By giving realistic delivery time frames up front you're going to save yourself a lot of grief and wasted emails trying to explain why customers haven't received their packages yet.

Remember—International customers really have you over the barrel. Tracking is virtually nonexistent for international shipments. The post office is experimenting with international delivery confirmation to select countries, but the service is spotty at best. There's no guarantee the mailman in Canada or the UK will actually scan your package when he drops it off. He may be having a bad day or he may be trying to outrun a dog. If your customer decides to file an item not received case you're going to lose because there's no way to provide proof of delivery.

Sorry to be the one to break it to you, but it's a fact of life when you're doing business on eBay. I've only had this happen once. A buyer in Germany opened an item not received case two days after paying for his item. There was no possible way it could travel from Iowa to Germany in two days.

Guess what? It didn't matter. eBay and PayPal decided the case against me because I didn't have proof of delivery. Like I said this happened one time out of five thousand international shipments so it's not a big deal.

One other quick comment here—many sellers assume proof of shipping is enough to win an international case. It's not. A stamped customs form from your post office is of no help to you if the buyer files an item not received case. If you can't show proof your item was delivered, you don't have a leg to stand on.

List on International Sites

What we've talked about so far involves listing your items on eBay.com, and making them available to buyers in foreign countries. The reason this works is eBay.com is the largest of the eBay sites and has the most listings posted to it. As a result many international buyers search here first when they're looking for new items.

If you do a lot of business with certain countries you may be able to increase sales there by listing items directly on that site.

If you're a registered eBay user you can sell on any of eBay's international sites. To get started just log in with your current ID and password, and start listing your items. Sellers with anchor stores can list on international sites for free. Sellers without an anchor store are charged listing fees if they exceed their free limits

If you want to make more sales there are a few details you should consider.

1. What language are you going to post your listings in?

If you're selling in Canada, the United Kingdom, or Australia—English might be fine. But, the UK and Australia use different dialects, and the meanings for words are not always the same. Canada has a large French speaking population so you need to consider them, too. Should you post in English and French?

If you're posting your listing in Germany, France, or Japan—what do you do? Many of the buyers there speak English as a second language, but do you want to leave their understanding to chance?

It's a tough call. You can use Google Translate or Bing Translate to write your description. The translations are usually stilted, and hard to read. A better choice would be to find a native language translator on Fiverr or odesk. They would be able to provide you with a more accurate translation.

If you're selling low dollar value or one-of-a-kind items the translation apps are going to be your most cost effective option. If you're setting up more expensive items you are going to sell over and over again, a good translator can help you create more professional sounding listings that will make more sales. Look at it as an investment in your success.

Other sellers choose to rely on translation apps that let potential buyers select the language they want to read the description in. eBay offers several of these apps that you can place in your item description. One app is called *One Hour Translation* and the other is *Translation for Worldwide*. You can read more about them in the app guide at the end of this chapter.

2. What about your title? Are the keywords and the context the same in German, Spanish, and other languages as they are in the United States?

Do you know what terms someone in Germany would use to search for an iPad, or a smart phone? When they're looking for a denim jacket, what other terms would they search on?

Your title is how potential buyers discover your item. If you don't know the local dialect or slang, how do you know the best words to use in your title?

Go back to item one. A translator fluent in the native language would be able to write the most appropriate title for your item listings.

3. What are you going to charge for shipping?

Do you charge international rates, offer free shipping, or split it somewhere in the middle?

Shipping is a key ingredient in determining how successful you'll be at international selling. The good news is items just about always make it to their destination. The bad news is sometimes international packages take forever to arrive at their destination.

When I listed items on the eBay.uk site several years ago I marked my items up a bit and offered free shipping. A funny thing happened—most of my items ended up selling to my regular customers here in the United States. It wasn't quite what I expected, but sales did go up.

After a month I switched tactics and offered a low cost international shipping option—five dollars, compared to the nine dollar rate I charged on eBay.com. Once I did that I started getting more buyers from the U. K.

Joseph Dattilo, founder of Virtualbotix, LLC, says –

"We offer USPS and UPS shipping providers and generally have First Class International, Priority International, Priority Express International, and UPS International as an option. Initially we only had First Class International as an option, but found that very few high value items sold, and we were contacted by dozens of buyers who demanded that we make other methods available.

"Since offering USPS Priority Mail International and USPS Priority Mail express International we have seen a dramatic increase in sales of items whose value is greater than $100. The interesting thing is that the boost to sales occurred, but the use of these more expensive services is still rather rare. Customers seem more likely to buy knowing they have the option to get it fast, but often still choose the most economical shipping method…"

The final takeaway is sellers can benefit from offering a larger variety of shipping options, even if their customers decide not to take advantage of them.

4. How are you going to approach delivery time?

Even if you explain that your item ships from the United States, many buyers aren't going to understand. All they're going to see is your item is listed on their home site—eBay.uk or eBay.de.

Shipping time is a tough call with any international shipping method. A lot of my First Class shipments make it to Europe faster than they do across the state. Others seem like they get buried on the proverbial slow boat to China.

The problem is, as a seller, you have no way of knowing which packages are going to get tied up in customs. The best you can do is help to set reliable delivery expectations for your customers.

Offer your customers a variety of mailing options—First Class International, Priority International, and Priority Express International, then give them time frames for delivery using each service. Tell customers the longest it should take for items to deliver. Most often their package will arrive sooner, and customers will be delighted because the item was delivered sooner than they expected.

5. Are you going to price your item in U S dollars, Pounds Sterling, or Euros?

If you're selling on eBay.uk or eBay.de and you price your item in dollars it's going to confuse buyers. If you price your item in Pounds Sterling or Euros you're going to have to keep a close eye on currency fluctuations to make sure you don't end up taking a bath if the market turns. When you go to pull your money out of PayPal, it's a two-step process. You have to convert your currency to U S dollars first, and then you can transfer funds to your bank.

6. What are you going to tell your customers about VAT taxes, customs fees, and duty fees?

Many customers aren't going to understand why they have to pay extra fees and taxes. When you list items on their home site they don't associate the purchase triggering additional fees for customs and duty.

To prevent negative feedback and multiple returns you need to explain in every listing that your item ships from the United States and customers are responsible for all customs and duty fees as well as VAT taxes. You need to include the same information in every shipping email.

Joseph Dattilo, of Virtuabotix, says they adhere to eBay's policy on every international listing and include the following disclaimer in every item description –

"For international orders (outside of the United States of America) please allow for additional time for your products to arrive, or choose one of our expedited services to ensure your product arrives in a timely manner. Basic international shipping can take as much as 30 to 60 days depending on your country while expedited international shipments have guaranteed delivery windows.

"Import duties, taxes, and charges are not included in the item price or shipping cost. These charges are the buyer's responsibility.

"Please check with your country's customs office to determine what these additional costs will be prior to bidding or buying."

All sellers should include similar wording in their international listings. If you don't include similar wording, eBay may decide a case against you if a customer opens a buyer protection case against you citing extended delivery times or additional fees for customs.

Open an International eBay Store

If you're serious about international selling, and have a target market in mind, it might make sense to open an international eBay store.

Let's say you're doing a booming business selling vintage concert t-shirts. Your two best international markets are Germany and the United Kingdom. You've just picked up a new line of custom printed t-shirts, hoodies, bikinis, and other apparel items. The new items are selling well to buyers who like the vintage look, but can't lay down several hundred dollars for a vintage t-shirt.

You know from experience the majority of customers who buy your vintage look apparel discover it in your eBay store. Sales in the U. K. and Germany aren't taking off, but your marketing intern had a light bulb moment—What if you opened local eBay stores in those markets so you could cross promote the vintage look apparel?

Bingo!

The best way to grow an international market is the same way you do it at home. Build an eBay store, and cross promote your items.

Set up a scrolling gallery at the bottom of every listing that features the vintage look apparel. Mention the vintage look apparel in every listing, and invite customers to explore your eBay store for more great deals.

Set up listing headers that feature the new items. Build a store front with clickable links to the new categories. Make it bold. Make it visual.

Use markdown Manager to your advantage. Offer free shipping occasionally. Discount a different category every week or every month. Set up promotion boxes to highlight your specials.

If you're setting up an eBay store in a non-English speaking country, find a translator to set up your listings and titles.

. . . .

An eBay store is a slightly more expensive way to sell international, but the payoff could be immense if you can make a go of it.

The key to success is to localize the store to each market you sell in, cross promote items as much as possible, and run frequent specials to build your brand.

eBay Apps to Grow Your Business

Apps can help you make more sales. They can help you manage different aspects of your eBay business such as bookkeeping, social media updates, blogging, translations, etc.

Apps can also turn your listings into a waste dump.

One problem I've encountered using apps on eBay is it's impossible to completely eliminate them if you choose to stop using the app. I used One Hour Translation at the top of my listing for a while. Several months later when I stopped using it, the visible part of the app was taken out of my listings, but it was replaced with a blank space where the translation app used to appear.

I had the same problem when I used a social media app. When I stopped using it, the app was replaced with a blank space at the top of all my listings.

The only way to completely remove the app is to go into each item description page and manually strip out the HTML code.

Best advice: Think hard before adding any apps to your eBay listings.

Currency Converter

By 3D Sellers

. Let's buyers calculate auction prices in the currency of their choice.

Blog Post

By PMIT Inc.

. This app turns your eBay listings into blog posts so you can share them across your social media sites.

Endicia Int'l. Advisor

By Endicia.com

. Gives you the info you need to manage your international shipments. Helps you understand international shipping requirements to various countries, rates for different shipping classes, and expected delivery times.

Ship Saver Insurance

By Inkfrog

. Discount insurance for international shipments. At the time of this writing (2014), you can insure USPS First Class shipments for $1.10 per $100 of value up to $1000.

My Store Maps

By My Store Credit, Inc.

. Place world maps in your item descriptions to show buyers locations you have previously shipped to. Some sellers say the visual representation encourages customers to order from them.

Webgistix GlobalFill

By Webgistix Corporation

. Allows sellers outside of the United States to print bar coded mailing labels for shipments into the United States. The claim is that the bar codes can reduce shipping time by up to five days.

One Hour Translation

By 3D Seller

. A translation widget you can add to your listings that supports up to twelve languages.

Translator for Worldwide

By PMIT Inc.

. A translation app you can include in your eBay listings. Currently supports 60 languages.

Interview with Joseph Dattilo on International Shipping

(This is an extract of an interview with Joseph Dattilo of Virtuabotix. They sell on eBay, Amazon, and from their own website https://www.virtuabotix.com/. Joseph is the founder of Virtuabotix, LLC, and handles much of the international selling for his company. His take on international selling should help both new and existing eBay sellers.)

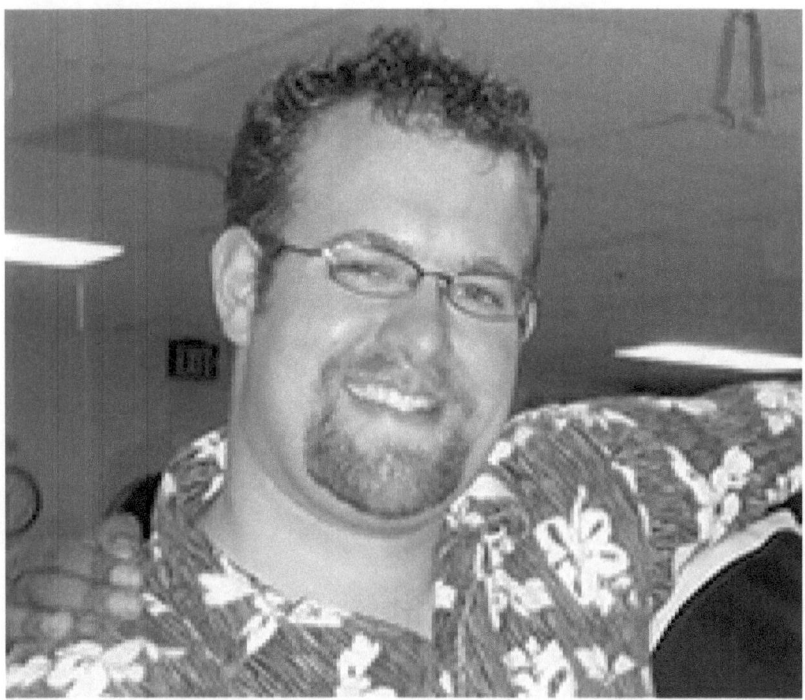

Joseph Dattilo

Could you tell me a little bit about why you don't use the Global Shipping Program?

By the time the Global Shipping Program was a consideration we already had started shipping internationally from both Amazon and our own Website. Because of the fees and other restrictions we opted to streamline shipping with our own process.

One problem I've encountered with the program is sticker shock for my customers. When eBay includes their fees, shipping charges, customs, etc. the price is often three or four times what I normally charge. Is that similar to your findings?

In our experience the lower cost we can provide as an option for shipping, the more likely we will make the sale. Increasing the cost to international buyers did not seem like a viable strategy since we are able to maintain less than $10 shipping rates for basic international orders by shipping and insuring directly. Our estimates placed the cost at well around the 2 to 3 times mark if we used the Global Ship Program.

One concern everyone has is tracking with international shipments. What shipping services do you use? What has been your experience with tracking, or do you even worry about it?

We offer UPS and USPS shipping providers, and generally have First Class International, Priority International, Priority Express International, and UPS International as an option. Initially we only had First Class International as an option. But we found very few high value items sold. We were contacted by dozens and dozens of buyers who demanded we make other shipping methods available.

Since offering both USPS Priority Mail International, and USPS Priority Mail Express International we have seen a dramatic increase in sales of items whose value is greater than $100. The interesting thing is the boost to sales occurred, but the use of these more expensive services are still rather rare. Customers appear more likely to buy knowing they have the option to get it fast, but most still choose the most economical shipping method.

Even if you pay for tracking, a lot of times you can't actually track your packages. Priority Mail Express International is completely un-trackable outside of the US (despite what is advertised by the postal service).

You mention international shipping is about 25% of your business? Are those numbers fairly consistent for you, or are they seasonal?

For our business there has always been a fairly large amount of international interest, so the ratio is fairly consistent regardless of time of year. The only time when that is not the case is during the holidays (October to January). US sales greatly increase on all channels during that time period.

Which countries are your buyers coming from now?

Canada, Australia, and most of the Euro zone countries perform fairly well. There's also a strong market in Brazil, Chile, and several other South American countries.

It is likely that our sales in Spanish speaking countries would improve if we made a Spanish version of our listings available.

Do you use eBay's international visibility program, or do you just enable international shipping?

We simply enable international shipping at this point, and we seem to be selling well in international markets.

You said you also sell on Amazon and from your own website. How do international sales from those sites compare to eBay?

International performance is very strong on eBay and Virtuabotix.com, especially when compared to Amazon. One reason for this is Amazon forces you to provide only two methods of international shipping. That means the only two options we can provide are standard, and the most expensive shipping option. This also makes it difficult to list things with LIPO batteries that have to have customized shipping rules and require UPS shipping (which is extremely expensive).

I know a lot of sellers who shy away from international shipping because of all of the horror stories they've heard about packages getting lost, stolen, etc. Do you have a big problem with international shipments going astray? or are your numbers similar to those for domestic packages?

International orders and customers can be as difficult as the stories make them out to be—sometimes. And, there are some problem orders, but when you consider only 1 in 200 orders tends to have problems (caused by the post office) it's still a fairly good track record.

We used to have a lot more problems with international customers, but that was primarily due to poor communications, and customers not having clear delivery expectations. Some of the worst situations with international order disputes were because it was not clear how long standard orders can take to deliver. Delivery can take as long as 30 to 60 days (It's always better to overestimate).

An even worse problem is first time international buyers who are outraged by having to pay VAT taxes and other import fees specific to their country.

In order to address a lot of those problems we put the verbiage below to help. The part about import duties and taxes is required to be inside your listing verbatim to fit the guidelines eBay requires to remove negative feedback that specifically relates to VAT & other Taxes or duties.

International Buyers – Please Note:

For international order (outside of the United States of America) please allow for additional time for your products to arrive, or choose one of our expedited services to ensure your product arrives in a timely manner. Basic International shipping can take as much as 30 to 60 days depending on your country while expedited international shipments have guaranteed delivery windows.

Import duties, taxes, and charges are not included in the item price or shipping cost. These charges are the buyer's responsibility.

You mention Spanish speaking countries would probably bring you more sales if you spent extra time on them. Have

you tried listing directly on those sites, or opening an international store in the countries you sell in.

We have identified some of our top markets, and would like to translate out listings and site into Spanish to help those customers use our products, and give greater levels of exposure in those countries. At such a time that we have those translations available we would likely create specific listings for those sites. We are also looking for distributors in those countries who can ship locally since that is often more desirable for individuals in those countries, and would reduce the impact of international shipping costs and delays on conversions for our products.

When you sell on international sites, is currency fluctuation a problem, or do you list your items in U S Dollars?

In general we list our items in US Dollars. Currency fluctuation has a greater impact on our cost of goods sold than it does on our per sale revenue. Ensuring our shipping prices are both reasonable, and adequate enough to cover all costs have a much more significant effect since shipping prices increase dramatically as weight and volume increases. It is easy to lose money if you do not set your shipping prices appropriately.

Despite what is advertised by the postal service international tracking doesn't always happen. Is that a problem for you as far as refunds and other customer service issues? Or do you just give a refund when a customer complains, and move on to the next sale?

Our responsibility to our customer does not end until our products have reached and satisfied the technical needs of our customers. Generally when a problem arises with international shipping where a product has not arrived and it is outside or near the maximum time range expected for the service selected, we simply send a replacement or refund the purchase as appropriate. It is very important to collect messages from your buyers with the statement that they never received your product, and to file a claim report as soon as possible providing this evidence to your insurance company in order for insurance payments to be approved. Failure to provide written proof of non-delivery or damage can cost you a lot.

Generally the idea is to make sure your customer knows you trust that they are having a genuine problem and that you are eager and willing to fix it. Ask for a confirmation of delivery address, and a clear statement of the un-delivered or damaged goods (a picture in the case of damage is often required). Finally you provide the replacement or refund as agreed upon between you and the customer. In the background, you will then submit a claim and wait the long period (often over 90 days) for your claim to be approved and paid. Trying to make one of your customers wait for the insurance to kick in is a recipe for disaster, after-all it's not their fault (even if it is :D).

eBay has had a number of self-inflicted problems over the last four months. Of course, they had the security breach for both eBay and PayPal, and have forced users to change their passwords. eBay also eliminated all of their Google AdWords this year, and soon afterwards they were busted by Google for practicing Black Hat SEO tactics. As a result Google removed a lot of eBay listings from search. How has this affected your business? Has it slowed sales, or caused other problems?

Because of our multi-channel approach an adverse effect on eBay has a positive effect on Amazon or Virtuabotix.com. An adverse effect on

Amazon has a positive effect on eBay or Virtuabotix.com, and you guessed it...an adverse effect on Virtuabotix.com usually results in a positive effect on eBay or Amazon.

Overall we have had a much more pleasant experience with eBay then Amazon, and we genuinely feel like eBay cares about having our products on their site. In contrast selling electronics on Amazon can be a nightmare, and we have had to spend a great deal of time and money dealing with Amazon policies that are designed more to benefit Amazon than anyone else. The ability to brand your business on eBay as compared to the outright banning of the practice on Amazon also plays a large factor in the value that eBay can provide to a business.

Overall despite any recent problems that eBay may have encountered, we at Virtuabotix.com still feel that our relationship with eBay has tons of potential for growth, and that the overall most Americans in need of our Electronics, and Robotics equipment have a positive view of the purchasing experience that shopping Virtuabotix through eBay provides them.

Customs Forms

The easiest way to handle customs forms is by using online shipping tools. When you use the online tools available through eBay, Click-N-Ship, Endicia, or Stamps.com they automatically walk you through the forms and ensure they are filled out correctly.

For those of you who insist on doing it old style here's a quick tutorial on customs forms.

The post office uses two customs forms—form 2976 and form 2976-A. Form 2976 is required on all international packages weighing less than four pounds. Form 2976-A is required for all international packages weighing more than four pounds.

Form 2976

Form 2976

The key information needed for each form is –

- Sender's address
- Recipient address
- Value of each item enclosed
- Total value of all items enclosed
- Description of contents
- Senders signature

You are given several choices to describe the contents including: gift, document, commercial sample, other. You need to check other, and then describe the contents in the description box.

Oftentimes sellers will ask you to lie about the value or check the gift box so they don't have to pay duty fees (taxes). Be aware that if you are caught doing this it is a felony—subject to fines and jail time. If you're tempted to fudge the form for them, ask yourself—is the extra sale worth the penalties you could face?

That's pretty much all there is to it.

Have the post office walk you through your first customs form. After doing it once or twice you'll be a pro and wonder why you ever worried about international shipping.

Form 2976 A

Form 2976A

Remember form 2976 A is for international packages that weigh over four pounds, or contain contents valued at over $400.

The key information needed to fill out form 2976 A is –

- Sender's address
- Recipient address
- Value of each item enclosed
- Total value of all items enclosed
- Description of contents
- Senders signature

You are given several choices to describe the contents including: gift, document, commercial sample, other. You need to check other, and then describe the contents in the description box.

Know Your Numbers

*(Much of this section was originally published in my book - **eBay Bookkeeping Made Easy**. It's a primer on bookkeeping, taxes, business types, and tax deductions. The information in this section can save you thousands of dollars on your taxes every year.)*

Get Organized

The first thing you're going to need is a system to organize and store your receipts and records. Some sellers use a file cabinet. Some use expandable file folders. I like to use loose-leaf binders. I get a five inch binder, monthly divider inserts, and storage pocket inserts.

Storing everything this way keeps all of my business records readily accessible, and the binder fits neatly on my bookshelf. I can store fifteen years of business records side-by-side in a relatively small space.

Save your receipts

Get used to it now. You need to save all of your receipts.

When you buy something on line, print out the invoice, punch it with a three hole punch, and store it in your three ring binder under the month of purchase.

Save all of your mortgage or rent receipts, utility bills, phone bills, cable bills, sewer bills, etc. Store them in a zipper pouch in your binder. You're going to need them to file for the home office deduction. It's going to save your thousands of dollars on your taxes every year.

If you purchase supplies at Walmart, Staples, Office Depot, etc. save your receipts in a No. 10 envelope. Label the envelopes by month and store them in a zipper pouch in your binder.

Write down your mileage

Go to Walmart, Target, or your office supply superstore and buy a mileage log. They cost about three bucks, and can save you close to a thousand dollars over the course of the year.

Starting today – You need to write down the beginning mileage on your vehicle. Every time you get in the car to run to the post office, pick up supplies, cruise a garage or estate sale, or anything related to your business – write it down. You need to record your beginning and ending mileage. Jot down a quick note about where you went, or why you went there. It doesn't have to be a novel or anything fancy. Post Office, bank, yard sale – just something to leave a trail of how it was business related.

Save all of your auto related receipts as well. The government lets you deduct your actual travel related expenses, or the mileage deduction (56¢ this year), whichever is greater. To ensure the largest deduction you need to save your car payment stubs, insurance payment records, gas receipts, repair bills, oil change receipts, anything related to your car. Grab another No. 10 envelope for each month, and label it auto expenses.

Claim your workspace

In order to claim the home office deduction we talked about earlier you need to devote a portion of your home exclusively to your online business. Pick a room, a portion of a room, your garage, basement, or whatever. Get everything not related to your business out of there, and start setting up your workspace.

Even if you do most of your listing sitting in the recliner in front of the TV you need a separate room for storage, mailing, and quiet time. The space your chair occupies doesn't count as a work area for the home office deduction and neither does the kitchen table if it doubles as a shipping center and a suppertime smorgasbord.

Open a business checking account

You're running a business now. One of the first things you need to do is separate your business and financial expenses.

Open a business checking account, and get a business debit card and credit card. This does two things. In case of an IRS audit, it shows them you are serious about your business. And two, it keeps you from nickel and diming your business to death. The minute you deposit your eBay money in your personal account you're going to start spending it on a Starbucks coffee, a Mickey D's burger, whatever. If you're ever going to accurately track your business earnings and expenses you need to separate it from your personal money.

PayPal is for business

Starting today, you need to make a decision that your PayPal account is a part of your business. Don't make personal purchases with your PayPal account. If you have a PayPal debit card, stop using it to buy pop, gas, groceries, etc. Use it when you pick up shipping supplies, or purchase inventory for your business.

When you do slip up and make a personal purchase with your PayPal account or PayPal debit card make sure you label it as a personal expenditure. That way it won't mess with your accounting records.

Set Money aside to expand your business

Once the money starts pouring into your account it's easy to get caught up in spending it. Decide up front that you're going to reinvest a certain percentage of your profits into expanding your business, whether that means adding new product lines, upgrading your computer system, or updating your work area.

Do this today, before the extra money becomes a part of your regular spending habits.

Make a plan, and work your plan

This one ties into setting money aside for business expansion.

After your business has been running for a while it's time to sit down and develop a business plan. Decide where you want to be in six months, a year from now, and five years from now. It doesn't have to be a lengthy document. You can start by jotting down a few notes – I want to double my sales over the next eighteen months, or by this time next year I want to be making $20,000 a year.

As time goes by add to your plan. Make it more specific. Make a list of short term and long term targets, and check them off as you reach them.

In short, make a plan, and work your plan.

. . . .

Bookkeeping should be an important part of your plan. Business success is measured by numbers.

You don't need to be an accounting genius to be successful selling online, but you do need to know enough to understand your numbers.

In the next section I'm going to give you a list of accounting terms that can come in handy. The more you understand them the better you will be at managing your business.

Here's the very least you need to know about accounting to run your business properly.

Accounting records are recorded in what's called a **general ledger**. It is basically a financial record of a company over a period of time. The information recorded in it is used by accountants and accounting programs to prepare financial statements.

Accountants use what's called a double entry system. A debit on one side is offset by a credit on the other side. The good news is with today's advanced software, business owners don't need to know anything about debits and credits. The program does all of the heavy lifting for you and crunches the numbers.

A **balance sheet** shows a company's assets, liabilities, and owner's equity at a given point in time. The simple formula behind the balance sheet is –

assets = liabilities + owner's equity

A **cash flow statement** shows all of the money a company earns and spends over a period of time. Company's use cash flow projections to help manage their spending, and ensure they have the required money on hand to cover their bills.

A profit and loss statement or **P & L statement** shows whether a business is profitable or not over a period of time. Companies generally prepare P & L statements monthly, quarterly, and yearly.

The general format for the P & L statement is to list income accounts at the top, then expenses, followed by a final line that shows the "bottom line" – or profit and loss.

If you understand these reports you will be more in tune with the financial health of your business.

Getting Started With GoDaddy Bookkeeping

GoDaddy Bookkeeping is available as an app you can download from eBay's applications bar. Amazon and Etsy sellers can check out the online version by visiting this link http://www.godaddy.com/accounting/accounting-software.aspx?isc=gooob012&ci=87249.

The service was originally known as Outright, and was taken over by GoDaddy last year. It's an online accounting solution that will serve the needs of most users. It automatically imports transaction data from your PayPal account, and posts it to the proper categories. Users can also synch their business credit cards and checking accounts with the service.

For sellers conducting business on multiple platforms GoDaddy Bookkeeping can import transaction data from eBay, Amazon and Etsy. It also works with several invoicing services including FreshBooks, Shoeboxed, and Harvest.

Here's the least you need to know. GoDaddy Bookkeeping is available in the *Applications* tab on your *My eBay* page. Hover your mouse over *Applications* until it shows Manage Applications, click on this and scroll through the list of applications until you come to *Outright*. Click on *Outright*, and select *Try it Free*.

GoDaddy Bookkeeping is available as a monthly ($9.99) or yearly ($99.00) subscription. Choose your poison and follow the prompts to get started.

Overview

The first page you see is your account overview. It contains all of the basic information about your account. In the upper right corner it shows your yearly profit or loss so you can tell at a glance where you stand. Below this is a graph that charts your income and expenses, a pie chart that shows your current month's expenses, and then a list of open invoices.

Below this is a section that shows Invoice Activity. Most online sellers aren't going to use this feature as all of your invoicing is done through eBay, Amazon, Etsy, and your ecommerce storefronts. If you're running a side business where your customers pay through PayPal this is where you would bill your customers for products or services sold.

In the left hand column you'll see four small blue boxes. The first box is labeled *New This Week* and tracks your new sales, and any uncategorized expenses. To view your new transactions or uncategorized expenses click on the number, and it will take you to your general ledger.

The *Money I Have Box* lets you view the balances in your accounts – PayPal, Amazon, and any bank accounts you have connected.

The Money I Owe box shows your liabilities or the money you owe. Some of the accounts shown here are your eBay balance, and money owed to Amazon and Etsy for seller fees.

The last box is labeled *Taxes*. It shows you several key tax indicators for your business. The first line shows your estimated quarterly tax payment, and when it is due. The mileage line shows your year to date mileage expenses. When you click on mileage it takes you to your general ledger and lets you log your mileage. The last line shows your *Sales Tax Liability*, so you always know how much you owe.

Below the four blue boxes you should see two blue bars. *Add Account* lets you add your various seller accounts, PayPal Account, and any bank accounts you want to tie into GoDaddy Bookkeeping. *Refresh All* imports data from your connected accounts so that you're viewing the most recent information available.

If you scroll back up to the top of the page you'll see your six control tabs – Overview, Income, Expenses, Reports, Taxes, and Manage. When you click on any of these they open more program options.

Before I describe the control tabs there's one other item I should cover. Sometimes a tan bar will appear just below the control tab. It shows program alerts or problems GoDaddy Bookkeeping may be experiencing with your account. When you click on the Fix It highlight it will walk you through solving the problem so you can get your program up and running correctly again.

. . . .

You can view your profit & loss statement anytime by clicking on the *view details* tab underneath where it says *(Year) Profit & Loss* on the GoDaddy Bookkeeping *Overview* page.

Your Profit & Loss statement gives you a quick overview of the financial health of your business. The top section shows your sources of income, and the bottom section details your expenses. The final line shows your "bottom line," or the actual profit or loss your business is making.

The default view for your P & L is the previous twelve months, but you have the option to change that any time you'd like. Scroll up to the top of the page under *Profit & Loss* where you see *ending.* You can choose the ending month or year, or you can change the time period to day, week, month, quarter, or year. To return to the chart select the chart icon on the right hand side.

If you want to take a closer look at a transaction all of the items on your P & L are clickable. Select the one you want to examine and it will take you to the general ledger page for that category.

Moving back down to the bottom of the page you will see two tabs at the far right side. Export lets you transfer P & L information to a Microsoft Excel file. Selecting print will give you a hard copy of your P & L.

Income

The income tab lets you manage your online income accounts. When you click on income it takes you to your general ledger page for income, and you can view your most recent transactions.

Once again, all of the transactions displayed are clickable. If you want to edit a transaction select it, and make the needed corrections.

What I recommend here is to set up categories for all of your income transactions so you can track where your money is coming from. When GoDaddy Bookkeeping imports income transactions it brings all of them in under the general "sales" heading. If you're just selling on one venue, such as eBay or Amazon, that's not a problem. If you sell across multiple platforms it's important to know the source your money is coming from. This way you can take corrective action if a sales venue is underperforming.

The first thing you need to know is every time you make a sale GoDaddy Bookkeeping records it as two separate transactions. The merchandise portion is recorded under the "sales" heading. If postage was charged on the transaction it is recorded under the heading "shipping income."

If you want to add additional sales categories select a transaction, and then scroll down the page until you see a heading labeled *Good to Know*. Over to the right hand side you will see a link labeled *Manage Categories*. Select it. This shows you a chart of your current income categories. To add a category select *New income Category*. Categorize it as *Business* or *Nonbusiness*, and then name the new category. After doing this you need to select a tax category. To tie the category you created to sales you would choose *gross receipts or sales*. Select *create*, and your new category is ready to use.

To give you an idea about how to use this, I added the following categories to my income account – eBay sales, Amazon, Bonanaza, *eBid*, bidStart, Kindle, Create Space, and

Audible. By doing this I can keep separate tabs on each of my sales channels. It gives me better control over my business, and allows me to spot patterns early as they're beginning to emerge.

After you set up your income categories you need to assign each individual transaction to the proper category. The easiest way to do this is from the Overview page. Select *view details* to see your P & L. Click on *sales* in the income section of your P & L. This will pull up all of your unassigned items. Select each item separately, and assign it to the proper income account. This step is pretty straightforward and should take just a few moments a day.

Whenever you're working on your P & L you also want to take a look at your uncategorized expenses. They're listed at the bottom of the P & L, just before you see your bottom line. Most items are categorized when they're imported, but there are usually a few uncategorized items, either because you purchased from a new supplier and GoDaddy Bookkeeping doesn't know how to classify it, or because the items you purchased from that supplier may fit into several different expense categories. Click on the individual unclassified transactions and assign them to the proper category.

If you do this every time you open your program it will only take a few minutes of your time, and it will ensure your P & L is up-to-date and accurate.

Expenses

When you select expenses it brings up the general ledger view for your business expenses.

Similar to the income category you can set up personalized categories to customize GoDaddy Bookkeeping for your business needs. Select an individual expense to enter the edit mode. Scroll down the page until you see the heading *Good to Know*. Move your mouse to the far right of the page and click on *manage categories*. Select *new expense category* and follow the prompts. Categorize the expense as a business or nonbusiness expense and name it. Scroll through the *tax category list* to tie your new expense to the proper category, and then select *Create*.

I would suggest setting up custom categories for your internet and cell phone providers, storage space rental, etc.

I find it useful to lump a few expense categories together. The main category I do this with is postage. I throw all of my shipping expenses in there – boxes, packing tape, stay free mailers, peanuts, you name it. The reason I do this is it makes it easier to compare my shipping expenses and shipping income. As long as the shipping income is equal to or more than my shipping expense, I know I'm on the right track. When they get out of whack it's time for an intervention to determine what went wrong.

With my other expenses my main concern is that they're consistent from month-to-month. If one month is way up without a similar bump in sales it's time to investigate what happened. Sometime it's a special purchase I had the opportunity to make; sometimes a number was entered wrong. The key thing is to watch your numbers and react quickly when you see that something is out of whack.

Reports

When you select reports it brings you to your Profit and loss statement. GoDaddy bookkeeping always shows you the chart first. Select *view as table* to see your P & L Statement.

If you're running a business you should know these numbers forwards and backwards. Growth is good, but I like to see consistent numbers across the board.

When I'm comparing my book sales numbers, the first thing I do is compare them with the last few months. If sales seem unusually low I take a peek at last year's numbers to see if it's a seasonal trend. You should do the same thing.

Online sales are always slower in summer. They normally pick up by late August and run strong through spring. February is a little iffy – it can go either way. The first half of November can be the same way waiting for Christmas buying to kick in.

Key point: Use your P & L to help forecast fluctuations in your business. Study it for trends, where sales are increasing or decreasing, or where expenses are rising. Put on your detective hat and figure out what's happening. Doing this will make you a better business person, and help your business to grow stronger over the long haul.

Taxes

The taxes section helps you with three specific areas.

1) It provides your Schedule C information to make tax time a breeze. Just transfer over the numbers and you're ready to file. Keep in mind you're still going to need a tax advisor or a good tax program like TurboTax Business or HR Block Business. GoDaddy Bookkeeping doesn't figure the home office deduction, tax credits, etc. They just provide you with the raw numbers to fill out your Schedule C.

2) GoDaddy tracks your sales taxes due, so it's easy to file and submit your state reports. As long as you have eBay, Amazon, and Etsy set up to collect sales tax in your state, GoDaddy Bookkeeping will track all of the information for you.

3) Every time you log into your account you are able to see your estimated tax payments and the date they are due. This way the due date and the amount you owe won't sneak up on you.

Manage

When you select manage it displays a list of all the accounts you have connected to GoDaddy Bookkeeping. If any of the accounts have errors you will see a tan bar displayed by them. Click on the blue *Fix It* link to take care of account issues.

If you want to connect more accounts, select *Add an Account* at the top of the page

. . . .

Good to know

You can easily reassign categories if something appears is mis-categorized.

Most often when this happens it's because the program does not recognize how to classify the transaction. To fix the problem select the item that needs to be classified. At the far right it will say uncategorized item, select the correct category from the drop down box, and press save.

You will also need to re-categorize items when you make a non-business related purchase. GoDaddy Bookkeeping has a *personal expense* category you can assign the item to so it is removed from your business records. If you sell a personal item and receive payment for an item through your PayPal account you can reassign it to the *personal income* category.

Best advice

Keep a close eye on your accounting program. Update it every few days. It's easier to catch errors when just a few items are displayed. If you let it go too long, a large list of items to re-categorize can seem overwhelming.

Keeping Records With a Spreadsheet

What if you want to keep track of your income and expenses the old fashioned way – using an Excel spreadsheet or a hand written ledger?

No problem.

If you use Excel you need to set up your income and expense categories similar to the way accounting programs do. It should look something like this –

Income

- eBay sales

- Amazon sales

- Etsy sales

- Bonanza sales

- bidStart sales

- Sales tax collected

- Shipping income

Expenses

- Cost of goods sold

- eBay fees

- Amazon fees

- Etsy fees

- Bonanza fees

- Internet expenses

- Phone

- Utilities

- Rent

- Computer equipment

- Software

- Professional fees

- Postage

- Mailing supplies

- Office supplies

Bottom Line

The easiest way to track your expenses is in a simple ledger style. Run your categories down the right hand side of the page. Put your days across the top of the page. Leave room to subtotal your income and expenses. At the very bottom you should have a space for your "bottom line" or profit and loss.

Assign a separate page for each month. At the end of each month transfer all of the information over to a page with yearly totals. Excel users have an advantage here because you can set these items to automatically update.

What I've outlined here is a very simple system, but it will give you all the information you need to manage your business. By looking over your income and expenses you should be able to spot trends and identify cash flow problems.

The best advice I can give you is to try to update your information every day or two. If you leave it go until the end of the month the task is going to seem overwhelming.

What You Need to Know About Taxes

Remember that old saying, "The only thing certain in life is death and taxes." Running a business is all about collecting and paying taxes.

Here are just a few of the different taxes you're going to be dealing with in your eBay business.

1) Sales & use taxes
2) Estimated taxes
3) Self-employment taxes
4) Unemployment tax
5) State and Federal Income Taxes

We're going to talk a little bit about each of these taxes – What they are? How they affect your business? And, what you need to do to stay on the right side of the IRS and your local tax authorities.

1) **Sales & use taxes**. Forty-five states require residents to pay a sales tax when they purchase property within that state. If you are an online seller and make a sale within your home state, you are required by law to collect the proper sales tax on it, and remit the payment to your state tax authority. Failure to collect sales

tax could put you on the wrong side of tax authorities if your sales are audited.

To collect taxes you need to apply for a sales and use tax permit (sometimes called a resale permit) from your state. There is normally no charge for it, but some states may require you to make a deposit based upon the volume of transactions you are expected to handle. You will be asked a few quick questions about your business, your sales channel, and your expected sales revenue. Once you receive your permit you are required to collect tax on every transaction you process in your home state. Most states base your payment period upon your expected tax collections. As a result you may have to remit payments monthly, quarterly, or annually.

Use tax is one of the most overlooked or misunderstood taxes. The way it's supposed to work is if you purchase something from outside of your home state and don't pay sales tax, you're supposed to fess up on your state income tax form and pay the appropriate tax. As you can probably guess, that rarely happens.

A good example of an item that would qualify for use tax is if you purchase your mailers from an out of state supplier on eBay. They ship them to you without charging sales tax. Because no sales tax was charged on this transaction when you purchased it, you are obligated to pay a use tax to make up for it.

The same thing is true for non-business owners. If you order clothes from a seller on eBay or Amazon and aren't charged sales tax you are obligated to declare the transaction on your state income tax return, and pay the appropriate sales tax on it.

If you intend to purchase items from a wholesaler they will require you to provide them with a state tax id. If you can't produce a tax id, some wholesalers will refuse to do business with you, others will insist on charging you sales tax on all of your purchases. You can also use your tax permit to eliminate sales taxes when you are purchasing items for resale from other retailers. So the next time you scoop up a cartload of closeouts at the outlet mall you can save yourself a bundle by not having to pay the sales tax.

2) **Estimated taxes**. If you are self-employed you are required to pay estimated taxes to the IRS and to your state tax authority. Quarterly taxes are due April 15, July 15, October 15, and January 15. Tax programs such as TurboTax and H R Block will help you estimate your quarterly taxes. If you use GoDaddy Bookkeeping it will show you your estimated taxes due. GoDaddy also shows your sales tax liability.

Keep in mind most of these programs estimate your taxes based on last year's income, or in the case of GoDaddy Bookkeeping they base their estimates on your trending income. If your income is sporadic or changes from year to year you may want to consult with an accountant or tax advisor to ensure you're paying in the proper amount.

If you pay in less than a certain percentage of the amount that is due you may wind up having to pay extra fees and penalties.

3) **Self-employment taxes** are similar to Social Security and Medicare taxes charged to people who work for an employer. The only difference is self-employed persons need to self-report these taxes, and pay both the employer's and the employee's share.

Self-employment taxes are figured on Schedule SE of your IRS Form 1040. In 2014 the self-employment tax rate was 15.3% - 12.4% for Social Security, and 2.9% for Medicare. In 2014 the amount of income subject to the portion for Social Security tax was capped at $117,000. There is no cap for the Medicare tax portion of self-employment tax.

You can deduct the employer portion of your self-employment tax (approximately 50 percent) when you figure your adjusted gross income for Federal taxes.

4) **Unemployment taxes**. If you hire employees to work in your online business you are required to pay unemployment taxes. These vary by state. Just keep in mind, there is a separate state and Federal tax due.

See Publication 926 for more information and a list of state taxing authorities.
http://www.irs.gov/publications/p926/index.html

5) **Federal and state taxes**. When most online sellers think about taxes, these are what come to mind.

Some online sellers try to avoid paying income taxes on their earnings, or think they're just for big time sellers. The truth is if you make as little as one dollar selling online you are required to report it for income tax purposes.

To keep everyone honest, the government imposed mandatory reporting requirements upon PayPal. If more than $20,000 is deposited into your PayPal account during the course of the year, PayPal is required to report it to the IRS on form 1099-K.

To view your form 1099-K sign into your PayPal Account, hover your pointer over the **history** tab, and this will bring up a drop down menu. You want to click on **tax documents**, and this will give you the option to view a PDF file of your 1099-K, if one was generated for you.

At this time you are not required to submit the PayPal 1099-K with your income tax filing, but you should be sure you are reporting at least as much income as is shown on it. You can be sure the IRS is matching them up, and taking a close look at your 1099-K, and the income you report on your tax return.

. . . .

That's the very least you need to know about taxes and you're online business. Here are a few more tips that can help you out when the time comes to prepare your Federal and state tax forms.

Business income is reported on Schedule C of your Form 1040.

Several tax programs are available to make filing your business taxes easier. The two I've had the most experience working with are TurboTax Business and H R Block Premium or H R Block Premium & Business. Each of these programs will conduct a fact finding interview with you about your business, and walk you step-by-step through filing your tax return.

If you pay extra for the premium version of GoDaddy Bookkeeping it will generate a paper version of your Schedule C with all of the information you need to key into your 1040 Tax Form. One other quick tip. If you don't pay for the premium version of GoDaddy Bookkeeping all of your information previous to the current twelve month will be hidden from your view. To ensure you don't lose any important financial data print a copy of your P & L, and your monthly statements before the end of January. If you don't, you will need to subscribe to the premium version to recover your information.

Even if you use an accountant or tax preparer doing your taxes first can save you hundreds of dollars when it comes time to file your taxes. This way all of the information is gathered together and entered in the correct areas on your tax return. All your tax professional needs to do is review everything to make sure there was nothing you overlooked or left out.

Most Common Tax Deductions

One of the perks of being a business owner is the ability to shift some of your income by taking advantage of various business deductions. Here are some of the most common business deductions taken by online business owners.

Home Office Deduction. Many business owners are afraid to claim the home office deduction because they've heard the IRS targets filers who take it. That's pretty much one of those urban legends that gets bigger every time it's told.

The home office deduction is every online seller's best friend, and can save you thousands of dollars on your taxes if you use it properly.

Here are the IRS rules for taking the home office deduction:

1) Your home must be your principal place of business.
2) You must use the area of your home (a room, or portion of a room) exclusively to conduct business. This means if you do all of your work at your kitchen table, you would not qualify for the home office deduction, because you don't use that area exclusively for business. If, on the other hand, you devote an extra bedroom, basement, or garage exclusively to conducting the activities of your online business then this space would qualify for the home office deduction.

To learn more about the home office deduction you can check out Publication 587. http://www.irs.gov/publications/p587/index.html

The methods for calculating the home office deduction changed in 2013, so even if you have taken it in the past you may want to brush up on the new guidelines.

Mileage Deduction. If you use your vehicle while conducting your business you are able to deduct your expenses. Business owners can take either the standard mileage deduction, or deduct the actual expenses incurred for the use of the vehicle in their business.

To take the mileage deduction you need to record all of the miles your car is driven for personal and for business use. I would recommend purchasing a mileage log. You can find one in the office supply section at Walmart or Target, or at larger office supply stores such as Office Max, Staples, or Office Depot. They run about $3.00, and are small enough to slip under your visor or into your glove box.

Each time you head to the post office, run to the store for mailing supplies, or to a yard sale or estate sale to pick up new inventory make sure to record your beginning and ending mileage.

In 2014 the standard mileage deduction was 56¢ per business mile driven. If you opt to deduct actual expenses, make sure to record all of your expenses for car payments, insurance, repairs, tires, oil changes, and gasoline. You can then deduct the percentage of expenses based on the miles driven for business usage.

Travel. Did you ever want to visit California or Hawaii, but weren't sure you could afford it?. The cost of travel is fully deductible as long as it is business related.

Let's say you're ready for a vacation and eBay is having one of its events in Scottsdale. You are able to deduct all of your expenses – airfare, car rentals, cabs, motels, food, and admission – as long as they are related to the event. If your spouse helps out in your business, their expenses would be covered as well. If you decide to make a real vacation of it and bring the kids along too, you would not be able to deduct expenses for their travel, food, lodging, etc. because they do not participate in the business.

The travel expense deduction can also be used to cover day trips out of town. If you visit an estate sale or auction several hundred miles away all of your expenses related to the buying trip would be deductible. Again, if you bring along the kids or someone unrelated to your business, their expenses would not be covered.

Computers, printers, office supplies. Are you a techie? Have you always wanted to own the latest, greatest gadgets, but wished you had a rich uncle to help you out with the payments?

Uncle Sam can come to the rescue here too. You can deduct the price of a new computer, printer, cell phone, iPad, or any other gadget that you regularly use in your online business. The only hitch is the item needs to be for your business use only.

You have the option of depreciating the expense of your purchase over the expected life of the item, or in most cases, you can deduct the full value of the item in the year it is purchased.

Internet, cell phone, etc. If you purchase a separate cell phone or internet service for your business you can deduct the full cost of them as a business expense. If you use them for business and personal use, you can only deduct the portion of the service you use for business.

If you're on track to make a little too much money this year and are worried about paying extra taxes, look at some of these ideas as ways to shift your tax burden. Once again, don't go crazy. Before you rush off on that junket to Hawaii or Europe, consult with your tax advisor first, to make sure the trip is deductible in your situation.

. . . .

Two other ideas while we're on the subject of tax deductions. You can use your business income to help fund your retirement, or to shift money to your kids by employing them to work in your business.

When you own your own business, you are allowed to fund a personal retirement account, 401K, SEP IRA, or KEOGH. The individual details are beyond the scope of this book; consult a tax professional for more details.

If you have kids, put them to work for your company and pay them the money you would have given them anyway. If you have college age kids, this is a good way of helping them pay their way through college while deducting the expense from your business. Keep in mind when you do this it is just like hiring a regular employee. You need to pay unemployment taxes, and provide a W-2 at the end of the year.

Business Permits, Licenses, & Such

Most eBay sellers run their businesses out of their homes. The majority of their neighbors don't know anything about it, except for the frequent comings and goings of the mail trucks, UPS vans, and Fed Ex guys.

As such, most eBay sellers don't bother with licenses or permits. They go about their daily routine pretty much unaware they may be breaking local codes and regulations.

What I'm going to do here is talk a little bit about the different licenses and permits a typical eBay business owner might bump up against, and give you a few tips on how to get them.

DBA (Doing Business As). If you conduct your business using an assumed (fictious) name you are required to record your information with the city clerk's office or county clerk's office depending upon where you live. Sometimes you can fill out the form online. Other times you will be required to go into the appropriate office, and pay a small fee. They check to see if the name is being used by another company in your area. If it is you will need to pick a new name. Banks will require a copy of your DBA if you attempt to open an account in your business's name.

Business License. Most cities and counties require a license to conduct business within their boundaries. The fees vary based upon the type of business you run. Where I live you apply for a license with the city's department of revenue. If you are unsure where to apply for a business license in your area Google "city name business license."

EIN (Employer identification Number). Most online businesses conduct their business using the owner's social security number. If you prefer not to share that information you can apply to the IRS for an EIN. Here is a link to apply for an EIN online https://www.us-tax-id-number.com/?gclid=CJaB3Kq_jr4CFckWMgod63cAbQ.

Home Business Permit. Some municipalities require homeowners to register if they are conducting a business out of their home. Call your city clerk's office to learn more about your areas licensing requirements.

Sales & Use Tax Permit. If you will be making sales to residents within the boundaries of your state you will be required to collect sales tax. Contact your state department of revenue for more information.

The SBA offers an excellent website covering local business licenses that may be required. They even have a search feature where you can enter your zip code, and it will return a list of business licenses and permits you may require. Follow this link for more details http://www.sba.gov/licenses-and-permits

Choose Your Business Structure

How you structure your business is an important factor in how much money you will keep at the end of the year.

Most eBay businesses will take one of the following structures.

1) Sole proprietorship
2) Partnership
3) Corporation
4) Small business corporation (Subchapter S)

Sole proprietorship

A sole proprietorship is the simplest form of business entity. It is run by one person with no distinction between the individual and the business. If the business makes money you keep all of the profits. If the business loses money, you are responsible for all of the losses.

Most sole proprietorships are conducted using the business owner's name. If you choose to run it under a different name you may need to file a DBA (Doing Business As). Normally you would need to register your business with the City Clerk's Office or a county office and pay a small fee. They will check to see if the name you want to use is already in use. If it is being used by another business you will need to choose another name.

Your business income should be recorded on Schedule C of your IRS 1040 tax form, and is taxed at your normal rate.

The major disadvantage of a sole proprietorship is you are 100% responsible for business liabilities. If you sell defective products or someone gets hurt on your business premises you are fully responsible and can be sued for liability.

Partnership

A partnership is a business relationship between two or more people. Partners normally sign a partnership agreement. Each of them contributes a certain amount of capital and labor, and shares in the profits or losses of the business.

Partners can share equally in the profits, or certain partners may have a larger percentage of ownership based upon the partnership agreement. Income is reported to each partner on a form called a Schedule K-1.

The disadvantage again is partners are fully responsible for any liabilities contracted by the business.

Corporation

A corporation is an independent legal entity owned by its shareholders. The business is registered with the State Corporation Department or Secretary of State's Office. They are required to have business licenses and permits, and to file quarterly and annual reports with the state they are incorporated in.

Corporations are normally owned by a large number of people who are issued shares in exchange for investing capital in the business.

Shareholders in the corporation receive income in the form of dividends. The biggest advantage of a corporation is income is taxed at a lower corporate rate, and liability is limited to the money you have invested in the corporation.

Subchapter S Corporation

Subchapter S corporations pass earnings and losses through to shareholders for federal tax purposes. Shareholders report income on their personal tax returns and pay taxes at their normal rate.

To qualify as an S Corporation the corporation must file Form 2553 Election by a Small Business Corporation. http://www.irs.gov/pub/irs-pdf/f2553.pdf

S Corporations have many advantages that make them attractive to online business owners.

1) Your assets are protected. The most you can lose as an investor is the money you have invested in the corporation.

2) Ability to reduce self-employment tax liability by paying yourself a portion of income as salary and as dividends.

3) Pass through taxation which allows owners to report losses or earnings on their personal tax returns.

4) It opens up new possibilities in offering yourself corporate perks such as better retirement plans, writing off college expenses, and other benefits. Be sure to consult with a qualified tax advisor before implementing any of these ideas.

Odds are most online businesses will begin life as a sole proprietorship and scale up as the business grows.

Sell Your Stuff Off of eBay

For most sellers eBay is the place to cut your teeth in online selling. The site is easy to use, they have a built in base of nearly 150 million eager buyers, and it's relatively inexpensive to get started.

The big four alternatives to selling on eBay are –

1. Amazon
2. Etsy
3. Fiverr
4. Personal website

Which one is the correct choice for your business depends upon what you sell, your sales volume, and your business goals.

If you sell any type of products Amazon is the clear choice for where to start selling next. If you sell handmade crafts or crafting supplies Etsy would be a good choice. If you sell services such as eBook covers, website design, white board videos, etc. Fiverr is a solid choice.

A personal website makes a good addition to selling on the above ecommerce sites, but as a standalone sales solution— it's not a good choice for most sellers.

The reason is the big ecommerce sites allow you to tap into their built in customer base and reach hundreds of millions of ready customers, a personal website is only as strong as your mailing list.

If you're just starting out that can be as few as ten or twenty customers.

Sell It on Amazon

A mazon is the 800 pound gorilla in the market when it comes to ecommerce.

Amazon and eBay ran neck-and-neck in sales for the year ending 2013. Amazon racked up $73.5 billion in sales; eBay came in at $76.5 billion (excluding auto sales). Amazon has 232 million registered users worldwide; eBay has 149 million registered users worldwide.

No other ecommerce sites come close.

If you're considering selling on another ecommerce platform, Amazon should be your first choice.

. . . .

Fees run about the same on both sites. The difference is eBay sellers pay listing and store fees to place their items on the site. Amazon sellers don't pay any listing or store fees (Amazon does have a Pro Merchant plan for $39.99 per month. It reduces the per item fee sellers pay when items sell, and lets sellers add new items to Amazon's catalog. I'll discuss this in more detail shortly.)

In most cases selling on Amazon is a matter of searching the site for a product similar to the one you want to sell. After you've located a similar product select the *Sell on Amazon* button below the buy box, and follow the prompts. Key items you need to supply are the condition of the item you wish to sell, and the price.

Unlike eBay, there's no need to upload pictures, create product descriptions, or write titles—for most of the items you're going to sell that information is already in place.

On Amazon, you're basically a hitchhiker on the item listing page.

Each product has one product description page. Buyers click on the price links to the item they're looking at and it brings up a list of sellers who have the product available and the price and condition it is available in.

. . . .

If you sell one-of-a-kind items not currently listed on Amazon you can create a new catalog listing for your item. Key points to remember when setting up a new catalog page include –

1. Personal branding is not allowed.
2. Descriptions should be product focused. Don't talk about your company, service, or selling policies.
3. Include product related photos. Don't include any company info in your photos.
4. Select your shipping service and price. Some categories, such as books, require you to select Amazon's shipping services and fees. In the book category $3.99 is the standard shipping fee Amazon will credit you when a book sells.
5. Set the product condition. If you're selling more than one item and they're in different conditions—list one item, and then select sell a similar item, and add the next one by describing the condition it is in.

Under Amazon's current terms of service all sellers can set up new catalog pages in most categories. A Pro Merchant Account gives you more flexibility.

The fee for a Pro Merchant account is $39.99 per month. For sellers who move more than forty items per month it'll save you some money. The reason is Amazon charges a 99¢ per item transaction fee for all items sold—Pro Merchant account holders aren't charged the fee.

Sell it on Etsy

When you mention Etsy what comes to most people's minds is crafts, but it's actually a whole lot more. A quick glance through the site will show you sellers offering to design websites, create blog themes, layout business cards, or draw custom made artwork.

If you plan to sell on Etsy you need to understand it's more of a community than eBay or Amazon. Buyers and sellers take time out to socialize and comment on each-others items. You can increase your chances of success by joining in the conversation.

Etsy is more folksy and down to earth. The first thing you notice is the look of their main sales page. It's more visual than the other ecommerce sites. When you view the category home pages there's no extra words, pricing, etc.—it's all visual. The entire page is nothing but product images with short descriptions under the pictures like shorts, pants, and prints.

When you click into a category you're presented with another page of illustrations dished up very similar to how you'd see them on Pinterest. The only text you're shown in this view is the title, the seller name below it, and the price.

The product description pages are bolder and more visual than those you find on eBay and Amazon.

At the top of the page there's a large picture of your item with arrow buttons that allow you to click through the pictures. To the right of the picture you'll find a product highlights box that includes, the title, price, product overview, and a buy button at the bottom where you can add the item to your cart.

Moving further down the page there's a more detailed description of the item, where you can tell more about it, or how you conceived and created the product. There's a large product gallery on the right side of the page that features some of your other items.

At the bottom of the page you can add a *Meet the Owner* section that includes a picture to introduce you to buyers.

. . . .

It's a totally unique shopping experience compared to what you find on eBay or Amazon, and to maximize sales you want to play to this difference.

Pictures are the key to making more sales. Spend extra time shooting the best pictures you can. Close up shots are best, especially of intricate design work. When you look at the clothing section the best illustrations have people modeling the clothes. Some sellers include full body pictures including their faces; others choose to cut them off at the neck. Another option would be to use a mannequin.

If you're selling smaller items consider investing in a light box. It will help you take better close up pictures, and get the lighting just right. You can find them online starting at thirty dollars.

The best descriptions are short. They should include a lot of white space and bullet points. I notice a lot of sellers give a short description followed by bullet points highlighting the key features of their item.

Other descriptions focus on the product. Sellers talk about what inspired their design, how they made it, and the materials used to make it. This is especially true with crafts and art prints, although I've noticed several sellers who use this method to talk about the designs on the clothing they sell.

My thought is if you're selling handmade items, crafts, or customized clothing or jewelry, you definitely want to make Etsy one of your seller platforms. If you offer graphic design or website services you can command a premium price on Etsy. The key to making more sales when you're offering services is to customize your pitch to crafters.

One of my books is called *Etsy Bookkeeping Made Easy*. It's a perfect fit to offer on Etsy. Another one of my books, *Sell it Online*, has a section on Etsy marketing so I will probably be offering it there soon, too.

For sellers offering crafting guides, patterns, and similar items, Etsy may be the perfect marketplace. They also allow digital downloads so you can enable instant delivery.

Sell It on Fiverr

Fiverr is a hip young website where buyers and sellers meet to exchange cash for services.

If you haven't checked it out yet, give it a look over. It's amazing what some of these folks will do for five bucks.

They have people designing WordPress sites, creating book covers, voice overs, drawing, cartooning, and creating banner ads. You name it, and someone is offering to do it—for five bucks—maybe.

Fiverr offers this amazing option that lets sellers bump that initial $5.00 purchase to $50.00, $100.00, or more. It's called Gig Extras, and you're gonna love it.

Let me tell you a little more about how Gig Extras work.

Before you can offer Gig Extras you must complete ten transactions with perfect feedback. After you do that you're allowed to offer limited Gig Extras. The next step is to level up and become a Level Two seller. This opens up more selling options, and gives you the golden ticket to charge more for Gig Extras.

The final step is to become a Top Rated Seller. These are the guys pulling in $40,000, $50,000, or more a year. The process for becoming a top rated seller is shrouded in mystery. These guys are voted in by Fiverr's Editors, and once in the club even more selling options open up to them including the ability to charge up to $100 for each Gig Extra.

Pretty cool, huh?

Now I'll tell you what a Gig Extra is. It's an option buyers can add on to their original purchase to enhance it. Let me give you an example. I purchase a lot of book covers. The cover design itself is $5.00. Most sellers offer a free image with your purchase, or they offer a Gig Extra for a premium image that will make your cover look even better. They charge $5.00 or $10.00 more for the premium image. If they subscribe to an image service it costs them 50¢ to $1.00, so that's an extra $4.00 to $9.50 in pure profit.

Another popular Gig Extra is to offer one day or two day service instead of the normal five to seven days. Buyers who want their item quicker pay an extra $5.00 to $20.00—all of it profit to the seller.

Other options are to upgrade to a Create Space book cover, or to order a PDF or PSD file of the cover art. The Create Space cover takes a few extra minutes to design but brings the seller an extra $10.00 or $20.00 in revenue. The PDF or PSD files don't cost the seller anything extra, they just need to send the existing file to the buyer.

Some sellers take a more unique approach to Gig Extras. They hang out a cyber-tip jar, and encourage buyers to leave a gratuity if they're happy with the product they received. Smart sellers leave detailed options for their tip jar. Check these out and see what you think.

1. For $5.00 I will get a Starbucks coffee to start my day.
2. For $20.00 I can pump half a tank of gas in my car.
3. For $50.00 I can take the wife and kids out for a nice meal.

4. For $100.00 I can invest in some new software to grow my business.

The bigger tips are few and far between, but when you hit one it's like winning the lotto.

That's the magic of Gig Extras. Most of them cost the seller no additional time or money, but allow the seller the chance to significantly boost their income.

Getting started on Fiver

The great thing about Fiverr is if you can imagine something, you can probably sell it there.

If it sounds like something that interests you I'd suggest spending a few days cruising around the site and exploring some of the stuff being sold on there.

Here is a list of some of the more popular gigs on Fiverr.

- Graphic Design. This includes book covers, business cards, banner advertisements, sales flyers, etc.
- White Board Videos. Most sellers offer a short thirty second video, and charge an extra $5.00 for each additional thirty seconds. Some charge more to add public domain music and images.
- Puppet Messages. Puppets are big on Fiverr. One of Fiverr's highest rated sellers is Professor Puppet. His videos have been used for internet advertisements, Kick starter campaigns, and more.

- Jingle Writing and Recording. Is music your talent? Lots of aspiring singers offer to record themselves singing your jingle. For an extra $10.00 to $20.00 they'll help you write it.
- Flyer Monger. Let's say you're like me and don't have any special talent. Many people have completed thousands of gigs doing nothing more than passing out flyers on busy streets, college campuses, and at major events.

Hopefully that's whetted your appetite to learn more about Fiverr.

The opportunity is there. You need to move yourself beyond thinking it's just five bucks. With a little ingenuity, a clever gig, and the right attitude—Fiverr gives you the opportunity to make real money doing what you enjoy.

To get, started visit http://www.fiverr.com/.

Sell it on Your Own Website

Selling from your own website is the ultimate thrill. You have complete control over design, product offering, and price. You don't have to pay eBay or Amazon their cut.

A personal website is also one of the toughest sells. Bringing customers to your own website is more painful than pulling teeth.

If you've got to have your own website, don't go it alone. Stick with a platform like Yahoo Stores, Amazon Webstores, or Shopify. They charge a small monthly fee and a per transaction fee for items sold, but the benefits are worth the extra cost— they're easy to set up, and let you tap into their customer base.

Here's a look at the big three web store solution providers—their features and prices.

1. **Yahoo Stores**. Yahoo offers a number of solutions for online entrepreneurs including stores, websites, and email solutions. I've used them all at one time or another and the great thing about them is they're easy to use, offer a large number of templates to choose from, and are fairly inexpensive.

The basic Yahoo store is $29.99 per month plus an additional 99¢ per month for domain hosting. You can upgrade to a Yahoo Pro store for $79.00 per month, or a Yahoo Premiere store for $299.00 a month.

You can check out more info about Yahoo Store at this link https://smallbusiness.yahoo.com/ecommerce.

2. **Amazon Web Stores**. Like Yahoo's online store solutions, Amazon's web store is easy to use. The nice thing about it is the interface is part of your regular Amazon account. It makes it simple to manage your inventory, and feature items both on your own website and on Amazon. The basic fee for a web store is $79.00 per month plus a two percent transaction fee.

I've had an Amazon web store in the past. They're easy to manage, design, and handle back office functions on. If you're selling on Amazon and want to open your own online store—this is the way to go. You can add your existing inventory to your web store with the click of a button. Amazon customers who discover you on that site can click on your profile to check on items in your web store, as a result you can benefit from cross traffic from Amazon.

You can get more info on Amazon Webstores by following this link http://webstore.amazon.com/.

3. **Shopify**. Shopify is a newer online store solution, but they're growing fast. They offer four different store solutions ranging in price from $14.00 to $179.00 per month plus a small per item transaction fee.

To be honest, I've never used their service. I did try the fourteen day free trial to set up a sample store. It was easy to set up and use. I had my basic design and first few items posted to it in less than an hour.

You can follow this link for more info on using Shopify http://www.shopify.com/. If you're serious about using Shopify you may want to check out a new book by Brian Patrick called Selling on Shopify.

If I was asked to give a recommendation it'd have to be the Amazon Web Store, especially if you're already selling on Amazon. The great thing is if you sell on Amazon, there's no extra learning curve for adding a website.

If you're not selling on Amazon, and you have a limited number of products to sell, the Shopify basic store for $14.00 would be an excellent way to build an ecommerce store front. Later as sales pick up and you add more products you could jump to a different selling plan.

Most auction listing services also offer a web store option. You can check with your hosting service for more details and pricing on their store options.

Other eBay Alternatives

There are a lot of smaller ecommerce websites catering to small and medium sized online sellers. Most sellers report mixed results selling on these sites. Often it boils down to the products you sell, and if you have an established clientele you can send to your storefront.

Four such services I've tried are –

1. **eCrater**. The best thing eCrater has going for themselves is they make it easy to import your items from eBay. Select <import your eBay products>, enter your eBay user id, and follow the prompts. They can't make it much simpler than that.

A big problem is they don't sync your inventory, so when items sell on either site you need to do it manually, or within a short time you're going to find yourself selling items you no longer have.

As far as sales go, I sell maybe five to ten items a year on eCrater. The traffic just isn't there—not for historical memorabilia anyway.

2. **bidStart**. This is another ecommerce site that makes it extremely simple to import your items from eBay. The other nice thing is bidStart has a service that will sync your inventory between the two sites. As a result you never have to worry about inventory problems.

I've been selling on bidStart for several years now. Like eCrater they're a nice site, they're easy to use, but the traffic just isn't there to make it pay off. I make maybe five to ten sales a year on bidStart.

3. **eBid**. I got started with eBid because for a while it was being touted as the next eBay. They ran a special where you could get started selling for $49.00, and not have to worry about more fees—ever. My eBay fees at the time were $1800 to $2000 a month so no more fees sounded pretty good.

Five years later I've made one sale on eBid for $12.99. That's a net loss of $37.00.

One of the problems is they don't have an eBay import tool. They ask you to download a spreadsheet and upload all of your info that way. It's totally beyond my technical level or the amount of time I want to spend with it. I don't see them growing or attracting a lot of eBay sellers until they develop an easy to use import tool.

4. **Bonanza**. I like the look and feel of Bonanza better than eBay. They have an easy to use import tool to bring your listings into the site. Bonanza also has a tool to sync all of your items across platforms.

What I like best about Bonanza is they went a step farther than the other ecommerce sites. They added Amazon and Etsy into the mix. Sellers with an Amazon Pro Merchant account can import their items from their Amazon store into Bonanza and sync them out to eBay. Sellers with an Etsy Shop can import their items to their Bonanza storefront and broadcast them to eBay.

I'm going to be honest, I've never made many sales on the Bonanza site itself, but since they've added the eBay connectivity feature my sales have shot up on eBay.

So here's what I'm going to say. Use Bonanza to manage your eBay and Amazon listings. Compared to other companies out there that perform the same services—Bonanza works cheap. Export Your Store charges $299 to move your eBay items to Amazon, and another $99 per month to keep them synced. Bonanza performs the same basic service for free if you're an eBay power seller. Amazon requires sellers to have a Pro Merchant account to access their API so keep in mind that's another $39.99 per month no matter which service you use.

To be fair, I need to add that Export Your Store goes one step farther than Bonanza. They export your items from eBay, and list them on Amazon. Bonanza only imports your Amazon and Etsy items into Bonanza, and then broadcasts them to eBay if you select that option. So if you want to move the contents of your eBay store to Amazon—use Export Your Store to perform the initial transfer. Then use Bonanza to keep your items synced. You can save as much as $99 a month in fees.

Bonanza has an excellent promotional program available to drive Google traffic to your listings. It's called the Bonanza Broadcaster. You can choose the percentage of your selling price you want to use for promotional fees—they range from 3.5% to 16%. The choices they offer for advertising your item include broadcasting it to Google Shopping, the Find, eBay, Nextag, and Bing Ads.

Promotion is an important consideration for eBay sellers now that eBay has cheaped out and stopped purchasing Google AdWords for their listings. It may even be more important since eBay was penalized by Google for Black Hat SEO tactics. Since early 2014 nearly fifty percent of eBay's listing have been penalized and removed from Google search.

For eBay sellers having your listings booted out of Google search is a real kick in the pants. It's brought many sellers to a standstill. Bonanza promotions are one way sellers can fight back.

Interview With Jason Bay of Bonanza

bonanza
everything but the ordinary

(I recently spoke with Jason Bay, Senior Product Marketing Manager with Bonanza about their export and promotional service. The information he gives can help eBay sellers decide if Bonanza can help them capture more sales on and off of eBay. Sellers should pay particular attention to the Bonanza Broadcaster service. It can help them pick up Google traffic after eBay pulled their AdWords program earlier this year.)

What should sellers do prior to importing their items from eBay or Amazon to help the import go smoother?

Bonanza's importer technology is built to handle any types of listings from the source marketplaces. We frequently update our importers as needed, so no preparation is required before doing an import.

Is HTML code in your listing a problem when importing items? I know Export Your Store strips out all of the code

when they import items (and sometimes parts of your listings as well). Bonanza doesn't do this. When I see eBay items I have imported to Bonanza they have all of the listing info in them as well as the original format - even if I originally used an Auctiva listing template.

No, HTML in the listings is not a problem. Our importer is very good about preserving HTML, images etc. I have seen some cases of particularly-complex HTML that it can't reproduce 100% accurately, but we believe it's the most reliable listing importer available. It can save a lot of time.

How does that work if you are exporting the item to Amazon? or do you just export items off of Amazon?

We do not export items from Bonanza to Amazon. Our Amazon link is a one-way link from Amazon to Bonanza. The Bonanza Broadcaster service publishes from Bonanza to eBay, Nextag, Pricegrabber, Google Shopping, Bing Ads, TheFind, and a few others that we don't mention by name. (In case I didn't explain that well, I'm attaching a quick sketch to hopefully clarify it for you.)

How many people have used your services to import / export items and do you have any statistics about their success selling those items?

Many thousands of sellers are using our importers on a daily basis. They generally do well in sales, because the Bonanza listings tend to rank highly on the search engines and comparison shopping engines (CSE's), especially after eBay's issues with Google this year. Also, sellers generally prefer to drive the traffic to Bonanza rather than eBay because Bonanza's selling fees are significantly lower.

(Courtesy of Jason Bay – Bonanza)

My experience has been that I didn't sell many items on Bonanza, but once I imported my items from Amazon and exported them to eBay the sales started rolling in. Is this where sellers should expect the most action?

If it's been several months since you last tried selling on Bonanza, you may have better luck nowadays. Our site traffic has continued to increase every year, especially over the past 9 months. We usually rank near the top 1,000 highest-traffic sites in the USA, according to Alexa.

Many new merchants are getting their first sales within 48 hours of listing their items, regardless of whether they're using the importers or the broadcasting service. But for the best action, opting into the broadcaster service to get access to the CSE's has seen good ROI for merchants.

For example, some of our more engaged sellers will regularly sell over 500 items per month even at the 6% ad commission level. Obviously that's not going to be the norm for every seller, but it does show that sellers can move a lot of product on Bonanza even without the higher commission levels.

What items sell best right now on Bonanza itself? or what categories are the most active for sales?

Some of the mega-categories for us include Lawn & Garden, Women's Fashion, Crafts, and Electronics. But we certainly see strong sales across categories. We have just under 10 million listings at this point, so shoppers come to Bonanza for a wide variety of products.

Promotional fees for Google and Bing ads can take a huge chunk of your sale. 3.5 % to 16% plus another 9 % or 10% to eBay for final value fees. Is it a good investment for sellers?

I think if a seller wants to be on both eBay and Bonanza, they'd do best to list their inventory on eBay and then use the "eBay daily sync" feature to automatically keep their Bonanza inventory in sync with eBay - that way, they don't have to pay fees on both platforms.

Note that the seller is in full control of which level of advertising commission they opt into, so if your product margins can't handle the higher percentages then you can choose a lower commission level. It's best if you can at least support up to the 6% level, because that gets your stuff published into Google Shopping, which brings a large amount of shoppers.

Also note that you usually won't be charged the full percentage for most sales: you'll only be charged for sales that directly originate from our advertising partners (not for Bonanza direct traffic), and even then it will often be lower than the full percentage since we usually don't have to bid at the max to get that traffic in the first place.

What kind of success are sellers having using your promotional programs?

Our advertising technology is very effective - it's one of the major reasons that sellers use Bonanza. Even sellers who are already doing well elsewhere will also sell their stuff on Bonanza to get access to the search engines and CSEs. We see the supermajority of sellers opting into higher commission rates because they continue to bump up their commission levels as they continue to see a strong return on the investment.

What percent of your sellers are taking advantage of the eBay program, and the advertising opportunities?

About half our sellers also sell on eBay. It's split between sellers that manage items on Bonanza and export to eBay, versus those that manage on eBay and import to Bonanza. It's just a matter of taste for which toolset the seller feels most comfortable with. As well, most sellers have opted into the advertising opportunities as their product margins allow. We do have many sellers in low-margin product categories that can't support the higher commission fees, but most choose to at least opt into the 6% level to get access to the Google CPC traffic.

Read These Books Next

eBay for Dummies by Marsha Collier. (Like all of the Dummies books, this one is a fun, easy read, and gives you a lot of great info to boot. You will find this especially helpful if you're new to eBay selling.

eBay 101: Selling on eBay for Part-time or Full-time Income by Steve Weber. Weber has written books about how to sell on all of the major online markets, eBay, Amazon, and Etsy. Another of his books, Barcode Booty, will show you how you can find items to sell in retail stores, thrift shops, library sales, and more, simply by using your cell phone and a barcode scanner.

eBay Power Seller Secrets: Insider Tips From eBay's Most Successful Sellers by Brad Schepp and Debra Schepp. This book helped me a lot back when I first started selling on eBay. A lot of the information is dated now, but you should still be able to pick up some useful tips.

Good Sellers, Bad Buyers: Protecting Yourself on eBay by Lexie Thornton. I just picked this book up during a free promotion last week. Learn how to protect yourself in everything you do on eBay from writing descriptions to shipping. I would strongly recommend this book.

eBay Photography the Smart Way by Joseph T. Sinclair and Stanley Livingston. This book will help you nail photographing any type of item for eBay. If you want to sell more items, better pictures are a sure way to draw more bidders.

How to Start and Run an eBay Consignment Business by Skip McGrath. This book is from 2006 so some of the information is going to be outdated, but if you are interested in selling items for other people, you can learn a lot from this book.

Easy HTML for eBay by Nicholas Chase. One thing that can help every eBay seller spruce up their listings is a basic understanding of html (the computer language used to build web pages). Another bonus is it's available for just one penny on Amazon.

Turn eBay Data Into Dollars by Ina Steiner. Ina Steiner, a co-founder of the eComerce Bytes Blog scored a homerun with this book. Once again, I have to tell you that some of the information provided is dated, but if you really want to understand how to apply data to auction pricing and selling, this is the best book available on the subject.

Tax Loopholes For eBay Sellers: Pay Less Tax and Make More Money by Diane Kennedy and Janelle Elms. Tax laws have changed since this book was published but it will give you a lot of ideas you probably never thought of about how your part time eBay business can help you save big money on taxes.

eBay Bookkeeping Made Easy by Nick Vulich. This is the only one of my books I'm going to recommend here. The reason I'm doing this is bookkeeping, taxes, and P & L statements are something that is foreign to most buyers. Unfortunately, if you don't understand the business end of selling on eBay it's nearly impossible to know whether you are making or losing money.

Creating an eBay Business Model: A Guide to Developing a Niche by Julien Powell. One of the keys to being successful selling on eBay that I emphasize in all my books is the need to discover your niche and cater to it. Julien Powell has written four or five good books about selling on eBay, and this is probably his best. It's a technical look at how to discover successful niches on eBay. It requires a lot of technical analysis and work with Excel spreadsheets, but if that's your thing—this book will help you locate your niche.

How to Buy Low on eBay and Sell high on Amazon by Jordan Malik. This book is a look at retail arbitrage (playing the price difference between two sites such as eBay). It's a fact certain items consistently sell for less on eBay than they do on Amazon, and vice versa. Smart sellers can take advantage of this anomaly to make a few extra bucks.

How to eBay in Real Life (For a Living) by Sam Rovin and Jason Richner. Not so much here about how to sell on eBay, more like stories from someone who has been there and done that. The authors have some good stories about different items they have sold, and different places they've sourced items from. You may also want to take a peek at their book, **How to eBay in Real Life 2: International Sales**. It's an interesting look at international sales, the things that sell, and what's involved in international shipping.

Before you go

Thank you for reading this book. If you enjoyed it, or found it helpful, I'd be grateful if you'd post a short review. Your review really does help. It helps other readers decide if this book would be a good investment for them, and it helps me to make this an even better book for you. I personally read all of the reviews my books receive, and based on what readers tell me, I can make my books even better, and include the kind of information readers want and need.

Thanks again for choosing my book, and here's wishing you great success in your writing.

Amazon page: amazon.com/author/nickvulich

Blog: http://www.indieauthorstoolbox.com/

Email: hi@nickvulich.com

Books by Nick Vulich

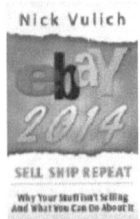

eBay 2014: Why You're Not Selling Anything on eBay, and What you Can Do About it

Freaking Idiots Guide to Selling on eBay: How Anyone Can Make $100 or More Everyday Selling on eBay

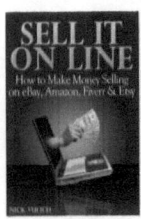

Sell it Online: How to Make Money Selling on eBay, Amazon, Fiverr, & Etsy

Audio Books by Nick Vulich

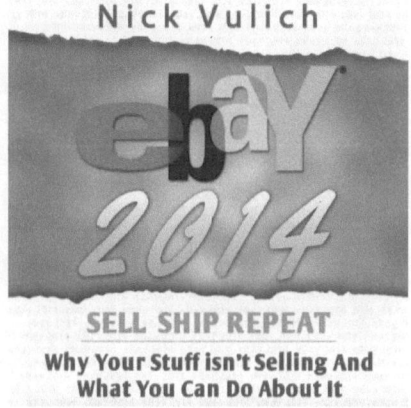

eBay 2014: Why Your Stuff Isn't Selling And What You Can Do About It

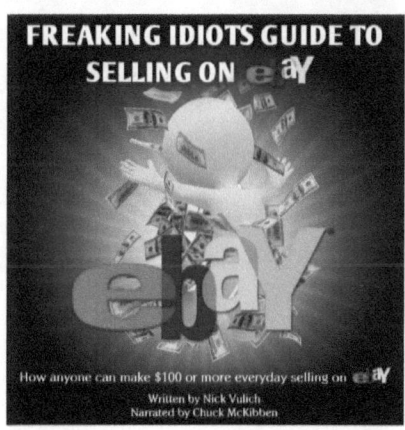

Freaking Idiots guide to Selling on eBay: How anyone can make $100 or more everyday selling on eBay

www.ingramcontent.com/pod-product-compliance
Lightning Source LLC
Chambersburg PA
CBHW021406170526
45164CB00002B/521